KING'S LYNN WRITERS

AN ANTHOLOGY

Published by:
Ashridge Press, Courtyard Cottage, Little Longstone, Bakewell, Derbyshire DE45 1NN
for:
King's Lynn Writers' Circle

ISBN 1 901214 21 4

© 2004 King's Lynn Writers' Circle

The rights of the members of the King's Lynn Writers' Circle
have been asserted individually by them
in accordance with the Copyright, Designs & Patents Act 1993

All rights reserved. No part of this publication may be reproduced,
stored in a retrieval system or transmitted in any form or by any means,
electronic, mechanical, photocopying recording or otherwise,
without the prior permission of the King's Lynn Writers' Circle.
Printed and bound by Antony Rowe Ltd, Eastbourne

CONTENTS

FOREWORD BY CHRIS GUTTERIDGE	7
MAGGIE ANDERSON	9
Moving On	10
Overheard in Passing	11
My Mother's Daughter	12
1967	14
Hand in Glove	15
Alternative History of South Wootton	21
Legend of Blackborough End	23
JIM BURCH	27
Nature Study	28
Spider in the Bath	30
Scene from the Train	38
Wide Awake Claire	39
Spatial Prejudice	43
So We moved to This Place	44
Rattling Lad	46
Daniel's Dream	49
Little Dolphin	52
CHRIS GUTTERIDGE	59
Irstead Shoals	60
One o' them Femernists	61
Stream of Consciousness	62
I bike up town most Tuesdies	63
Acle Bridge to Thurne Mouth	64
Darren's on the Hinternet	65
Leziate	66

We got new neighbours agin	67
Shakespearian Limerick & Learian Sonnet	69
Our New Rector	70
Sailing	71
Eternal triangle, Principle, Elevating, Discovery	72
The Wishing Stone	73
GINA GUTTERIDGE	77
My Mother	78
Fish, Turtles, Flowers	81
Glitterbug	83
Old Hunstanton Beach	84
Solace	87
The Eyes Have It	88
Black Magic	89
LINDSAY GUTTERIDGE	93
Butterfly	94
Olson	97
Symphony for cupboard doors and a light bulb	99
PAMELA PALMER	101
Daughter of the Forest	102
Halfway House	109
PATRICIA WALTON	117
Woman on the Beach	118
A Game of Chance	126
VAL WILSON	131
A River runs through it	132
First and Only	133
Gunman in the Hedge	137
Resurrection	138

Collaboration	142
Reverie	143
Crystalline	148
Tentacles	149
Soul-clamped	150
Rock Bottom	152
On Devolution	155
Rural Autumn	156
Wetland Miscellany	157
Sitting with Stella	158
My New Romance	162
PAUL WINSTANLEY	165
On the face of it	166
Candle in the Dark	169
Food for Thought	174
Elverford	180
Groundless Force	190
Prickly Problem	194
Safety Valve	197
Deadlier than the Male	200
Paintballs and Flowerbaskets	206
A Cover-Up Job	209

King's Lynn Writers' Circle
Gratefully acknowledge help and sponsorship of this publication from:

The Borough Council of King's Lynn and West Norfolk
Bernard Matthews Foods Ltd.
The Matthew Hodder Charitable Trust

EDITORIAL NOTE

Editing this anthology has been a privilege, a labour of love and an impossibility. The variety of pieces available defied any simple categorisation, so in the end I decided not to try.

Instead, what seemed to me to be the best of each author's work, whether light-hearted or serious, is grouped under his or her name, prefaced only by a photograph and a brief biographical note.

Of one thing I am certain. There is something for everyone. Dive in and enjoy!

Paul Winstanley

FOREWORD

King's Lynn Writers' Circle has been meeting on the second Thursday of every month for over twenty years, and I have been a member for about ten. During that time writers have come and gone, but throughout I have been impressed by the outstanding quality and diversity of their writing. This anthology of short stories, articles and poems, edited by Paul Winstanley, showcases many of our present members' work and demonstrates that the same high quality and diversity is still there.

Amongst our members past and present are professional novelists, published poets, journalists, authors of technical books, and those who write purely for their own pleasure and that of their friends in the circle. All are equally welcome at our relaxed monthly meetings, where we read our work to each other and discuss it in (I hope) a friendly and helpful way. Writing is a lonely occupation, and we all appreciate the chance to meet and talk with like-minded people.

We hope that you will enjoy reading this anthology as much as we have enjoyed writing it, and if you are a writer yourself, and live within reach of King's Lynn, we would be delighted to welcome you to our meetings.

Visit our website at www.lynnwriters.org.uk or ring 01553 630442 or 675463 for further details.

Chris Gutteridge, Chairman.

MAGGIE ANDERSON

Norfolk born and bred, Maggie has lived in King's Lynn for the past fifty-six years. She may be remembered as the voice of local radio on BBC Radio Norfolk, alongside 'Bruther Will' on Keith Skipper's 'Dinner-Time Show' or as the author of various contributions to the much-missed magazine 'On-King's Lynn.' For several years she was local correspondent for South Wootton, writing for both the E.D.P. 'Mercury' and the 'Lynn News.' She has written an as yet unpublished novel but is a published poet.

Maggie has been a member of Lynn Writers for longer than anyone, including herself, can remember.

MOVING ON

'I hope you don't mind me calling back,' Dave Roberts smiled apologetically. 'But if it's convenient, I'd like to take another look around.'

I invited him in. Admittedly he could have picked a better time; I had been busy preparing our evening meal. He moved about, upstairs and down, rapping on woodwork and opening and closing cupboard doors while I hovered behind him. The silence felt awkward. I tried to fill it.

'It's structurally very sound.'

'Uh, huh.'

'Needs a bit of updating, that's all.'

'Uh, huh.'

'It's very economical to heat.'

'Mmm.'

When he finally turned to me, he was smiling.

'Yes, I like it. As I can pay cash, I'll offer one thousand below asking price.'

My heart leapt with joy but I managed to keep my voice calm.

'I'm happy with that.' I offered my hand and we shook on the deal.

'When were you anticipating completing?', he asked.

'I already have another place, so as soon as possible.'

'Great. I'll let my solicitor know.'

As soon as I had seen him out, I rang Caroline.

'Guess what? I've sold it.'

'That's wonderful. And Susan?'

'It's all right, Caro. My wife doesn't suspect a thing.'

© 2004 Maggie Anderson

OVERHEARD IN PASSING

The most important advice ever given to budding authors is to observe and to listen, and then to take notes. From these humble beginnings are spawned a plethora of plots, characters, stories and, ultimately, novels.

But the observing and listening can bring its own rewards. Overhearing the conversation between two elderly ladies nattering away to each other in my local Post Office was a good example.

'Well, that's my pension got,' one remarked. 'Now I'm going over to the off-licence to buy my stockings.'

Was it time to get my hearing tested, I wondered? Surely that couldn't be right? It was, I learned later. Apparently the off-licence had diversified into other lines, and stockings were now offered for sale along with Saki and Sauternes.

On another occasion, a car pulled up beside a woman who was waiting impatiently in the street. She opened the passenger door and leaned over. From the raised voices, it was obvious that she was arguing with the driver. Finally she straightened up, folded her arms and firmly stated, in broad Norfolk, 'Well, if I'd 'a known yer wuz going ter go afore yer cum, I'd 'a cum with yer.'

And I gathered she intended making him go again, taking her this time.

But I'm still pondering on the conversation which I overheard on Market Day. Two old boys, one using an ancient bicycle to hold himself more or less erect, were chewing the fat in the centre of one of the aisles, completely blocking the way.

'How yer bin keeping then, ol' mate?' asked the one without the bike.

'Ah, well,' came the reply. 'Oi can still get me leg over, and as long as I can do that, Oi reckon Oi'm orl right.'

I'm trusting he meant over the crossbar!

© 2004 Maggie Anderson

MY MOTHER'S DAUGHTER

Memory is a strange thing. Months may pass without it casting up so much as a single thought about a particular person, and then a scent, a word in conversation, maybe even the season of the year rolls back time. Long ago shadows pad out, become flesh and live again. So it is with Mary. As each year draws to a close, I need only catch sight of the Nativity Scene, see Joseph standing protectively over a sky-and-white clad Virgin and Child, and once again I suffer the pangs I once felt as my classmate Mary, wearing a nightdress beneath a blue dressing gown, tenderly cradled a swaddled doll on centre stage of our primary school Nativity play.

Mary was always chosen to play the Virgin, partly because of her given name, but mainly because her public persona was that of a gentle and shy maiden. Yet out of sight and sound of parents and teachers, Mary redeemed herself in my eyes by being as mischievious as the remainder of her class mates.

I was in my first term at school when Mary entered my life. At first, experiencing myself as a newly individual entity, full of the self-importance of my own blossoming ego, I saw Mary not as a person but as a colour, a soft brown hue. Immediately I thought of her as a mouse, or else a young fawn; a timid dainty creature crying out for the sanctuary of a safe haven within a wicked world. Her very slightly wavy hair was a rich glossy deep brown, parted on one side and caught back in a brown slide. Her skin was the shade of very milky tea, not a sallow greasy Mediterranean skin, but smooth, blemish free, creamy brown. But her most noticeable features were her eyes, large expressive pools of velvety brown, seemingly holding within them the accumulated feminine wisdom of centuries past, so dark they were almost black. My mother took to her from the very first moment.

Our mothers were friends, that friendship born of mothers waiting together in rain and in shine each day at the school gates, at first only nodding, then discussing the weather, then more intimate matters, until they became bosom pals. And so Mary became a frequent visitor to my home, often invited to stay and have tea, not as my guest, but as my mother's. I tolerated her presence patiently, merely observing, with an amazed detachment, the change in my mother's manner while Mary was there. Until the evening of my sixth birthday. It was then that I was able to name the expression in my mother's eyes as she gazed down into Mary's sweet brown face. It was total and unconditional love.

The overwhelming jealousy which ravaged me at that moment is with me still, albeit subliminally; so is the deep sadness at the knowledge that I could emulate Mary in neither looks or temperament. Where she was rounded, I was thin, stick-like, gawky. Mary's gentleness only served to emphasise my own spiky, permanently defensive attitude. Yet even a few days later, when my mother snapped at me, in a fit of rage at some childish defiance, 'I wish Mary was my daughter, and not you,' I could direct no anger towards Mary. It was not her fault that she was a well-fed little brown mouse. Rather it was mine that I was not.

Now, fifty years on, it is Christmastide once again. I meet Mary's parents in town. Her mother greets me. I ask after Mary's health.
   'She's well,' I'm told. 'And just as pretty as ever,'
   My throat closes.

© 2004 Maggie Anderson

1967

How often I've wondered, just where did it go?
That soul-inspired feeling from so long ago.
We were Children of Peace back in 'sixty seven,
Transforming the Earth to our version of Heaven.
We sang songs of Love, wore flowers in our hair.
Preached Peace, not war, tried to show how to care.
But then:-

> The Ethos grew chill. Dreams withered and died.
Violence reigned. Greed became King,
And the hearts of the Peace Children cried.
Now the years slip away as we grow old and grey
And sadly look back on the past.
We had been young and strong. Our ideals were not wrong,
So why could we not hold them fast?

© 2004 Maggie Anderson

HAND IN GLOVE

Great Aunt Caroline's off-white kid gloves added the perfect finishing touch to Emma's Dickensian costume. Even so, her mother was still in two minds about lending them to her.

'Look, sweetheart,' she said, for what seemed to Emma like the twentieth time that day. 'I realise that tonight is very special. It's a great honour to be picked to sing, and I know you have to wear gloves, but these ones are irreplaceable. You will be careful, won't you. I'd hate anything to happen to them.'

Her father, shuffling uncomfortably in his best suit, winked at Emma.

'Sheila, she's fourteen, so stop fussing. And come along, or else we shall be late for the service.'

Her mother began to head towards the door, her back stiffening. 'It's all very well for you,' she sniffed. 'She was my Great Aunt, and she treasured those gloves. You know she did.'

In the car, Emma asked, 'So who exactly was Great Aunt Caroline?'

'She was my mother's mother's aunt. I didn't know her very well, but I remembered being taken to see her when I was a girl. She was a sweet old lady, but very old fashioned in her ways.'

'How?'

'Well, I was never allowed to use her first name. She was brought up to consider it very bad mannered. I always had to call her 'Great Aunt West'.' She smiled wistfully. 'And she always smelled of Eau de Cologne.'

'So is that what that faint scent on the gloves is? I thought it was lavender. But she's dead now, isn't she?'

'Yes. She died when I was about five months gone with you. Poor old soul, she was well into her nineties by then.'

'So she never even saw me.'

'No, she didn't. But that last time I visited her in hospital, when she was rambling and only semi-conscious, she suddenly opened her eyes, looked straight at me, and then said, as clear as can be, 'I like Emma.' So when you turned out to be a girl, that's what we called you.'

A short time later, Emma's parents dropped her off at the side entrance to All Saints church, and drove off to park the car. Emma, dressed in her Dickensian finery, complete with the kid gloves, lifted her skirts and made her way along the path towards the church in the wake of other choristers.

The gravel path leading up to the church's south door wended its way between gloomy ancient yews and the pale rectangles of the tombstones of long departed townsfolk. At its midway point, a single cast iron lamp standard, which had illuminated the path for as long as there had been street lighting in the town, threw out a welcoming circle of light, a haven in which to catch the breath before plunging back into darkness. At the foot of it, with her back to Emma, stood a slightly younger girl than herself, also dressed in costume, her dark hair caught up in a loose chignon.

'Hello. Are you singing tonight?' Emma asked as she drew level.

The girl sniffed, turning her face away.

'Yes,' she replied, her voice muffled.

'Hey, what's the matter. Why are you crying?'

The girl turned around, dabbing at her eyes with a tiny lace handkerchief.

'I've lost my gloves,' she whispered. 'And I'm on the very front row. Everyone will see.'

'Can't you hide your hands?' suggested Emma, then, 'Silly me, of course you can't.' as she realised the impossibility of her suggestion, for everyone had been thoroughly drilled until holding their hymn books up in a uniformly straight line was second nature.

The younger girl had turned into the light, so that Emma could see the undisguised misery in her face.

Impulsively she began to tug at the fingers of the gloves, saying, 'Then you must borrow mine. They smell a bit, but it's only some old scent. I'm right at the back, so I'll probably get away with it.'

But...'

'No, I insist. I'll say I forgot them. No-one will be particularly surprised. Scatty little Emma, that's how everyone describes me. I'm always forgetting something or other. What's your name, by the way?'

The other girl's tears had almost stopped. She gulped, and managed a watery smile.

'I'm Louise. Would you really do that for me? After all, we are total strangers.'

Emma grinned.

'As they always say, the show must go on, and your need is certainly greater than mine.' Her smile faded, and she laid her hand on Louise's arm. 'But you must promise me this. Louise, please, whatever you do, please, please, don't lose them, dirty them or damage them. They're a sort of family heirloom and my mother will go absolutely crazy if anything happens to them.'

Louise smiled gratefully as Emma pressed the gloves into her hand.

'I promise I'll be careful. And I'll never forget your kindness, not as long as I live.'

'Just don't forget the gloves and go home in them.'

'I won't, I promise. How does my face look?' She turned her

head towards the light.
'Not too bad. A splash of cold water, and you'll look fine. We'd better be getting inside. We don't want to be late.'
'Go on ahead,' said Louise. 'The pins in my hair feel loose.'
'Are you sure? You don't need any help?'
'No, you go. I'll find you as soon as the service is over.'

She gave Emma a brief hug, then began smoothing her hair, tucking up stray tendrils and adjusting the pins.

'See you later then.'

Emma turned and began walking towards the church, lifting her skirts clear of the gravel. At the next bend in the path, she paused and looked back. Louise was still against the lamp post, dabbing at her face.

'Don't be long,' Emma called. Louise raised her hand to show that she had heard and began putting her handkerchief into her bag.

Ahead of her, Emma could see light coming from the open church door. The organ burst into life, as the organist began playing a medley of seasonal music, to encourage the congregation to settle into their seats, and stop chattering. The choirmaster was standing just inside the door, urging laggards to hurry.

'Come along, Emma. Hurry up. I might have known that you would be late. Get to your place quickly. We are almost ready to start.'

Hastily Emma put her coat in the cloakroom, and took up her position. The interior of the church had been decorated with an abundance of fresh flowers and greenery, and lit only by candles, to give an authentic nineteenth century atmosphere. As the service began, Emma forgot everything but the music, and the sense of being an important and integral part of something beautiful, even ethereal. Not even a nudge and an angry frown at her bare hands from her neighbouring chorister could break her concentration.

The service ended, and the congregation slowly filed out. The choir began to chatter excitedly and mill about, thoroughly pleased at its performance, as Emma went in search of Louise. By the time she had reached the bottom of the steps, where the front row had been standing, the choir was beginning to disperse, and Louise was nowhere to be seen. Emma hurried to the cloakroom as fast as her full length skirts would allow, and grabbed her coat, then stood in the doorway to wait, but Louise did not pass her. The choirmaster was the last to leave.

'Still here, Emma?'

'I'm waiting for Louise.'

'Well, there's no-one else in there now, except for the Rector. I don't think I know Louise, she must have been a last minute substitute. There were quite a few. Now I hope you're not on your own. I trust your parents are meeting you?'

'Oh, yes, they're waiting for me on the market square.'

'Then I'll walk with you as far as the gate. It's a bit eerie in the churchyard, especially this late at night. Perhaps your friend has gone on ahead and is with your parents.'

Knowing that that was impossible, and beginning to feel slightly sick with anxiety, Emma let herself be guided along the path. She was convinced that she had lost the gloves. She began berating herself for being so foolish as to lend them to a complete stranger, and her stomach churned with anxiety as she imagined what her mother would say.

Her parents were waiting for her at the gate.

'That was lovely, Em. I'm so proud of you.' Her mother gave her a hug. 'But you feel very chilly. Come on, let's get you home and into the warm.'

As they drove, Emma gazed silently out of the window, praying that the car would pass Louise along the road, but her prayers went unanswered.

'Are you all right, Em? You're very quiet,' commented her mother.

'Over-excited,' said her father calmly. 'I think we could all do with a mug of hot cocoa and an early night.'

Despite the cocoa, Emma slept badly. Louise filled her dreams, holding the gloves just out of reach, snatching them away as Emma's fingers brushed against them. She woke early, her head throbbing, and got up to take some aspirin.

'Are you all right, Em?' called her mother.

'Yes, just a headache.'

'Come in here, let's have a look at you.'

Emma went into her parent's room. Her mother sat up in bed.

'You do look very flushed, dear. Are you coming down with something?'

'No, I don't think so. But, Mum, I've done a terrible thing. I'm really sorry, but I think I've lost Great Aunt Caroline's gloves.'

'No, you haven't,' replied her mother reassuringly. 'Dad found them in the car last night, after you'd gone in. The box is on the dressing table. Look.'

'But that's just the box,' Emma wailed. 'The gloves aren't inside.'

"Well, they were last night.'

Her mouth felt dry as she picked up the box, and gingerly opened it. Inside, carefully wrapped in tissue paper, lay the gloves.

'How did they get there?' she shrieked.

Her father stirred. 'Wassa matter?' he mumbled.

'Nothing, dear. Go back to sleep. Our dimwit daughter thought she had lost Aunt Caroline's gloves, that's all.'

Emma had flopped down on the dressing table stool, and was unwrapping the gloves. Gently she began easing one onto her hand, then stopped. There was something inside it.

'What's this? It wasn't here yesterday.' She took out the scrap of yellowed paper carefully. It was so old that the folds were disintegrating, and the ink was badly faded. She had to hold it close to the lamp to decipher it.

Her voice trembled as she read the neat copperplate handwriting aloud.

'My dearest Miss Emma, I tried to return your gloves after the service, but was unable to find you. I shall never forget your kindness. Very affectionately yours, Caroline Louise West. December 1909.'

© 2004 Maggie Anderson

AN ALTERNATIVE HISTORY OF SOUTH WOOTTON
a bit of Norfolk squit from Maggie Anderson

Long time ago, round about the beginning of the Middle Ages, several itinerant salters established a small community some three miles north-east of Lyn Episcopi. Orthodox access to this new village was by way of the Geywode Causey, a raised roadway which had been constructed across marshy ground to provide the heavy horse-drawn traffic of the day with a more or less firm and dry surface. However the inhabitants of the as yet un-named village, being both hardy souls and also fiercely independent, objected to using the five mile long meandering track to the town. Instead, most preferred to make their own way by the shortest possible route, despite the fact that this course of action led them directly across a couple of miles of the most treacherous tidal salt marshes imaginable.

One particular young man, who, because of a speech impediment, was considered to be the village idiot, became tired of having cold, wet and muddy feet each time he went into town. He was an inventive sort of chap, and so he made himself a pair of waterproof knee-length boots. Having previously heard of an article of clothing made from a similar material, which protected the head and neck, and was known as a Sou'Wester, he decided to call his innovation the Sou'Footer.

Keen to show off his new boots, he took them down to his local hostelry, which has for all time been known colloquially as the 'Mucky Duck', where his friends were drinking. They had considerable difficulty in understanding what he was saying, due in part to his speech impediment, but mostly because of the liberal quantities of ale which they had consumed.

Eventually he managed to convey his message to them, although they never did grasp the correct name of the boots, instead corrupting it permanently to Sou'Thwooters.

The new footwear caught on rapidly, and soon all the villagers were wearing them. Their young inventor became so proficient at making the boots that, although many tried, no-one else was ever able to equal the quality of his. Soon people were coming from miles around in order to purchase the genuine articles, and so the young man had 'Sou'Thwooter' signs erected by the wayside to direct strangers to his workshop. As the village straddled the busy road between Lyn Episcopi and Rising, he also had more signs put up to let people know that they were leaving the famous place where Sou'Thwooters were made. They read, 'No'Thwooter'.

Sou'Thwooters were subsequently made and worn in the village for centuries. In fact, it is widely accepted that whilst on a short visit to the locality, the Duke of Wellington witnessed several villagers squelching across the common to the 'Mucky Duck' in their Sou'Thwooters, and was thus inspired to commission the very similar boot which later bore his name.

Sadly, with the coming of the motor car, and the subsequent construction of the Northern By-Pass across the salt marsh, the manufacture and wearing of Sou'Thwooters passed into the annals of history. But it is certain that they will never be forgotten, for they became immortalised when the village was finally named, for it became South Wootton.

And, I hear you asking, what became of that other village, the one where there were 'No Thwootor'? What else, but North Wootton.

© 2004 Maggie Anderson

THE LEGEND OF BLACKBOROUGH END

Horry thought that he had been born in 1829, but his parents weren't admitting it, as that was the summer in which they had been married. In any event, 1847 saw him bored with the simple peasant living which he eked out in the valley of the River Nar, near to the village of Middleton. Fired by youthful enthusiasm, he bade farewell to his tearful mother and resentful father, and set out westward, intending to seek his fortune.

Four and a half years later he was back.

"Tha' wern't half a queer place, that there Cally-forn-ya," he commented to his closest crony, as they leaned on the five barred gate of his father's field.

'Welt, you din't cum back empty handed, no-how,' his friend replied. 'Yer got two o' the finest dickies I ever sin.' And he gazed in undisguised envy at the beautiful soft eyed black donkeys grazing close by. 'Wot yer call em?'

'The stallion, 'e be Jack,' replied Horry, 'And the mare be Jenny. Funny thing is, when I bought them, they wuz selling another mare and she be Jenny, too. Hin't got much imagination, them thar Americans, if they name all dickies Jack and Jenny. And guess wot, they call dickies burras. Now if that int a daft name, I dunno what is.'

'Silly ol' fules, seems like they don't even speak English proper. But what did you do with yerself, out there all alone? I did hear there was gold jest waiting for someone to pick it up off the ground in Cally-forn-ya. Did yer find any yerself?'

'Yeah, I found a bit. A few ol' boys did real well. I made meself a camp down river of one on em, and I sorted through all the spoil what came down from his place. Got quite a few ounces, enough to put something by, and pay the fare home for me an the dickies. Couldn't leave them behind, they bin good to me, and anyway, Jenny's in the family way. Be kinda hard, knuckling down to work here agin though.'

But knuckle down he did. Some folk hinted he'd brought a lot of gold home with him, envious of the way his family began to prosper, although his parents always denied it, saying only that their crops were doing so well that they fetched premium prices at market. Then they bought more land, and grew more crops, and grew ever wealthier.

When, during the following Spring, Horry married, his wife worked alongside him in the fields, while the donkey stallion carried loads and pulled carts that would have exhausted the strength of a much larger draught animal.

The mare had given birth to a filly foal, whose coat was as black as those of her parents. As she grew to maturity, another small black filly joined the family, and then another. Local donkey stallions sniffed the air and hew-hawed their approval. A few broke loose and came visiting during the night, and the donkey family grew, with the foals of aunts and uncles and cousins gambolling in the fields surrounding the farm.

Horry's family grew also. His one daughter was a well endowed and generous girl, and before too long, her generosity had provided her with a daughter of her own, whom they named Millicent.

Horry was enchanted by his little grand daughter. He bounced her on his knee, and sat her on the back of one of the quieter donkeys, and told her tales of the far away and long ago magical place called Cally-forn-ya, where the sun always shone, where the rivers ran golden with precious metals and all the dickies gloried in the names of Jack and Jenny Burra.

'And that ol' fella there,' he indicated the greying and knock kneed donkey who was dreaming away his last few months in the Norfolk sunshine.

'He is my first Jack Burra. He was with me when I panned for gold in Cally-forn-ya. He came all the way home with me, him and his missus. He founded this big herd of black dickies. And he is the one who made our family rich.'

'How do you mean, Grandfa Horry?'

'Never you mind, little mawther. The story isn't for ears as young as yours.'

But of course Millicent repeated the story at school, and her classmates went home and repeated the story to their parents, and everyone puzzled over the riddle of how Jack Burra had made Horry's fortune.

'It's gold,' they whispered. 'It has to be.'

Horry's little empire grew larger. He added mushroom sheds, and more fields, and finally a grand mansion for his entire family of aged parents, wife, daughter and Millicent.

'Grandfa Horry, what shall we name the house?' Millicent asked as it neared completion. 'It's got to have a name, Grandfa.'

Horry smiled. 'I've spent a lot of time thinking on that, and I've come up with a good 'un. I'm going to call it Blackborough End. After all, that's what made us all so rich.'

'How come, Grandfa?'

Horry leaned on the gate and gently pulled his hand up the nearest donkey's furry ear.

'I reckon you're old enough now to understand, gal. You know enough about what makes things grow well, and you know that what grows well, sells well. From there it dun't take too much working out. So, what colour are our dickies?'

'Black, Grandfa.'

'And what did I tell you they called them, back in Cally-forn-ya?'
'Burras, Grandfa.'
'So this is...?' Horry pointed to the donkey.
'A black burra.'
'Well done, gal. That's exactly it.'
'But what about the other word? The end. The end of what?' wailed a still uncomprehending Millicent,

At that moment a nearby donkey emitted a loud fart and deposited a large pile of waste matter on to the ground.

'Jack Junior's just gon an told yer hisself,' Horry laughed. 'That end.'

© 2004 Maggie Anderson

JIM BURCH

Born in London, Jim Burch has lived in East Anglia for the last 38 years. Though evacuated several times, once to King's Lynn, his school years were spent mainly in London during the Blitz, the doodle-bugs and the V2 raids. He has worked as a teacher, educational psychologist and university lecturer. His publications include, 'After October', a book of poems, and an illustrated booklet for children. One of his scripts has been made into a film by a local group. The stories included here were all aimed primarily at children but have given pleasure to many adults.

NATURE STUDY

I was evacuated three times during the war,
Once, with a brother to Kent,
Then, with brother and mother and aunt and cousins
To Norfolk,
Then, by myself,
Away from the Elysium of Brancaster,
To King's Lynn,
To Grammar School.

I made my own first, grubby, academic marks
And worshipped sportsground heroes.

One day I met one of these,
With his local girl,
Or rather, they met me
Fishing for tiddlers.

I displayed my catch, proudly.
'What's that?' they enquired, kindly.
'A stiggleback,' I replied, promptly.
'Stiggle? Stiggleback?'
(Oh fie! Oh fie! Oh la!)
They laughed.

Under a blue sky, in a meadow, on a warm day,
Ripples of laughter, simple as breath....
And they went their way.

I was puzzled merely
And thought to check my facts.

Later, the memory ceased merely to puzzle.
The riddle cracked
I would hear my chirping voice,

Then hear the gentle mimicry of theirs.
Feel my face burn,
My tongue lurch clumsily,
Feel small and squat and crouched.
Urchined, cockneyed,
Smelling of London and wet beds,
Scabies, impetigo, fleas.
Know innocence's decease.
Feel life give way to art.
Notice the sullen thudding of my heart,
And, dully, acknowledge pains
In all my growing parts.

© 2004 Jim Burch

THE SPIDER IN THE BATH

Sophie and Tom were brother and sister. Sophie was the older, and most people agreed that she was also the more sensible of the two. Tom, they would say, was a likeable lad, but one who seemed to think that the only point in having rules was because it was so much fun to break them.

They had been having an argument about how spiders got into the bath. Tom was sure that they always came down from the ceiling. Sophie was equally certain that they came up through the plug-hole. Neither would give way, so they decided to ask extra-granny.

Extra-granny was a very old lady who lived in a tiny, ramshackle cottage, not far from the children's home. Most people in the village regarded her as a witch, and kept out of her way. Sophie and Tom also thought that she might be a witch, but this only made her more interesting to them, so they secretly adopted her as an extra granny. Delighted to find herself with two such lively and talkative grandchildren, even though they were only extra-grandchildren, extra-granny was much more friendly towards them than she was to anyone else in the village, though even when a witch is being friendly, she often sounds grumpy and strict.

'This time,' she said firmly, 'it is Sophie who is right. Spiders get into the bath from the plug-hole.'

'That cannot be,' said Tom, who never minded arguing with anyone, 'because I always leave the plug in the plughole.'

'The spider pushes it out,' said extra-granny.

'These spiders are too small to push the plug out,' said Tom confidently, very pleased with himself to be winning the argument.

'Listen young man,' said extra-granny, 'it is not the spider you see in the bath who has pushed the plug out, but his MUCH BIGGER BROTHER SPIDER who has pushed the plug up for him.'

Sophie and Tom's mouths fell open, and their eyes became very large.

'And another thing,' continued extra-granny, 'do not ever kill a spider you find in the bath, because, if you do, that same MUCH BIGGER BROTHER SPIDER who helped him into the bath will come, during the night, through that same plughole, and seize you and carry you off.'

Both Tom and Sophie were pale, and shaky, and quiet, and thoughtful when they left extra-granny's cottage. They walked towards home in silence for a while. Then Tom's face cleared and he said, 'I don't believe her!'

'Why not Tom. Why not?' asked Sophie, who always became a little anxious when Tom was in one his defiant moods, like now.

'Because it's not possible, that's why,' said Tom, with great certainty.

'But extra-granny has never told us a lie,' protested Sophie.

'Well, she has this time,' said Tom firmly. 'Listen. Tell me this. How could a spider, big enough to carry me off, get through that small plug-hole, especially with those bits of metal which go across it? Tell me that.'

When they reached home, Tom marched straight up to the bathroom. Sophie followed close behind him, fearful of what he was going to do. There in the bath was a spider, quite a small one. Tom leaned over the bath.

'Don't. Please don't,' begged Sophie.

But without pausing Tom picked up the spider, pinched it between his fingers, and threw the small body out of the open window.

'Oh dear,' wailed Sophie, 'why do you never believe anything anyone tells you?'

'I don't believe nonsense,' said Tom. 'And that story was nonsense. I'm going to bed. If you don't find me in the morning, you'll know that I've been carried off by MUCH BIGGER BROTHER SPIDER,' and with a snort of laughter, Tom went into his bedroom and closed the door firmly behind him.

Sophie thought about telling her parents, but she knew that they would be more inclined to side with Tom than herself. They would also be angry that the children had been talking to the witch, as they called extra-granny. So, with a sigh, the sort of sigh that older sisters always give when they are worried about naughty younger brothers, Sophie too went to bed.

Now, I would have agreed with Tom (though I wouldn't have killed the little spider). Some things seem simply impossible. But Tom was wrong, and so would I have been. During the night things happened exactly as extra-granny had predicted. One moment, in the bath, at the plughole, all that could be seen was just a short length of hairy leg poking through. The very next minute, there in the bath and almost filling it was MUCH BIGGER BROTHER SPIDER. In no time at all, he had, with all eight hairy legs, stepped out of the bath and moved quickly and quietly into Tom's bedroom. (Spiders don't seem to notice doors).

Tom had been sleeping quietly, but he soon woke up when the spider seized him in his great hairy spider jaws, and carried him into the bathroom. The next moment they were in the bath, and the very next moment after that, even though Tom was wriggling furiously, and flinging his arms and legs about, they had disappeared down the plug-hole.

Sophie, wakened by a sound, jumped out of bed and, fearing the worst, ran into Tom's room. Tom's bed was empty. In the bathroom the plug in the bath was pushed out and, very faintly, from the plug-hole, she could hear Tom's voice crying out, 'Save me Sophie! Save me!'

Sophie could think of only one sensible thing to do. She quickly slipped on some clothes and shoes, went quietly to the front door, opened it, and ran down the dark street to the home of extra-granny.

Luckily extra-granny was still up, and opened the door straight away when she heard Sophie knocking.

'Oh! That foolish boy!' she said, when she heard Sophie's story. 'He deserves whatever that spider decides to do to him.'

'Oh no he doesn't!' said Sophie, with a vehemence which surprised extra-granny and Sophie herself, 'Tom is a foolish boy, but he is not a wicked one. We must save him. What will the spider do with him?'

'Well, I don't know for certain,' said extra-granny, 'but what he usually does is to tie the bothersome little person up in yards and yards of finest spider silk, until they can wriggle and shout no longer. He then usually hangs the cheeky little pest person up by a thread from the branch of a tree, for about 24 hours. And then..... .' Extra-granny paused and rolled her eyes around in their sockets.

'And then what?' demanded Sophie.

'Well, then he usually eats them,' said extra-granny, 'and serve him right I say, for ignoring my warning. He always was a most wilful boy.'

'Oh dear! Oh dear!' wailed Sophie, 'I must save him.'

'And how are you going to do that?' asked extra-granny.

'I don't know,' said Sophie, 'but first I must find some way of getting down that plug-hole. Can't you help me, instead of spending all your time criticising poor Tom? After all, he is your sort-of grandson. A proper granny would be worried, and trying her hardest to help.'

'Would she?' asked extra-granny, as though quite surprised to hear this. 'Hmmmm ..,' she thought and frowned so hard that her eyes crossed. 'There might be a way... but, if I tell you... and you do come back...you must promise to cut off all your golden ringlets and give them to me.'

'I promise,' said Sophie at once, 'gladly I promise. Now, tell me, what must I do?'

'Listen carefully,' said extra-granny. 'Half fill the bath so that, when you get in and lie down the water reaches your chin, but does not cover your nose. You must keep your clothes on and your eyes tight shut. Then, holding this magic charm in both hands, use your big toe to grip the chain and pull out the plug, and do not open your eyes again until you have counted slowly to twenty.'

'And then?' asked Sophie.

'Why, then it is all up to you,' replied extra-granny. She pushed something into Sophie's dress pocket, something else into her hand, gave one of her loudest cackles, spun round a few times, and disappeared, leaving Sophie clutching what turned out to be a dried out frog's leg.

Sophie was just about to throw this away in disgust when she realised that it must be the magic charm so, in spite of her distaste, she held on to it very tightly.

Unlike Tom, Sophie did exactly what extra-granny had told her, even though she did feel very foolish lying in the bath of water with all her clothes on, clutching a disgusting, dried frog's leg, and with the chain of the bath-plug wound around one of her big toes.

She closed her eyes, pulled out the plug and .... felt nothing at all. When she had counted slowly to twenty (well, actually, she counted to twenty two, just to be on the safe side), and opened her eyes, she found herself standing, soaking wet, on a path, in what appeared to be a large, very untidy garden.

'What now?' she wondered. But she did not have to wonder long for, there in front of her, on the path, were lots of wet spider's footprints, leading further down the garden.

'It's a good job spiders have eight legs,' she thought, 'it means that there are lots of prints to follow. It is also a good thing that I followed him so quickly, otherwise the sun would have dried the prints and I'd have had no idea which way to go.' Even as she looked at the prints, some of them began to fade. 'I'd better get a move on,' she thought, and hurried quickly down the path. Then another thought struck her, 'It is also a good job that it wasn't raining.'

The trail of damp footprints lead eventually to a dark place behind a garden shed. As she crept cautiously into this gloomy space, between the back of the shed and a line of trees, she could feel lots of fine strands of web brushing her face. She shuddered, but pushed on until there, right in front of her, wriggling slightly and making faint squeaking sounds, she could see a shape, something like an Egyptian mummy, hanging from the branch of a tree, just as extra-granny had described.

It was only now that Sophie discovered that what extra-granny had thrust into the pocket of her dress was a small pair of scissors. 'Good old extra-granny,' she thought, 'I hope Tom will remember to be grateful if we ever get away from here.'

Sophie found that, even standing on tip-toe, she could not reach high enough to cut the thread which hung down from the tree, so she started at the bottom of the wriggling shape, and cut slowly upwards.

At first a foot appeared, wearing one of Tom's school shoes. As she went higher a pair of rather grubby knees appeared. 'Those are definitely Tom's,' she thought. Next she reached some trousers, a belt, and then two hands, the fingers faintly moving. Finally, she could see a face, the dear, dear face of her tiresome brother Tom. He seemed to be half asleep at first, and to be content to stay where he was, drawing in deep breaths of wonderful-smelling fresh air. Then his eyes opened, and when he saw Sophie, he gave a great, happy smile.

'Hallo Sophie,' he said. 'I knew you would save me. Gosh, it's disgusting in here. I could hardly breathe. Why are you all wet?'

'No time to explain now,' said Sophie, helping him down, and leaving the now empty bag of silky threads hanging limply from the tree. 'It would be even more disgusting to get ourselves eaten by that spider. We must get out of here, though I'm not sure how. We'd better start by going back the way I came.'

The spider's footprints had all dried out by now, but Sophie's, though shrinking rapidly in the sun, were still just visible. They ended at a small puddle, which Sophie recognised as the pot where she had first found herself in the garden.

'Oh dear,' cried Sophie. 'Extra-granny was very helpful about telling me how to get in here, but said nothing about how we get out again.'

'What is that absolutely vile object you have in your hand?' asked Tom.

'It's a dried frog's leg,' said Sophie.

'Ugh!' shuddered Tom, 'throw it away.'

'No!' said Sophie, clutching the leg more firmly. 'Extra-granny gave it to me. It's a magic charm. Somehow it got me through that plug-hole, and down here, into this garden, so that I could find you.'

'Well, use it again to get us out of here,' said Tom. 'Come on Sophie, it's worth a try.'

'Right,' said Sophie. 'Hold my hand. Now close your eyes. Now, with me, count slowly up to twenty.'

For once, Tom did as he was told, with no questions and no arguing. But when they opened their eyes, they were still in exactly the same spot. What's more, from the bottom of the garden they could hear a rustling sound, the sort of sound you would expect to hear if a giant spider, a MUCH BIGGER BROTHER SPIDER, was pushing its way through the trees and bushes towards them.

'Try again!' shouted Tom.

Sophie clutched the frog's leg even more tightly and pleaded, 'I really will keep my promise about giving you my ringlets.' Tom looked at her in surprise to hear this. But they were still in the garden, and now, between the branches further down the garden, great hairy legs could be seen, moving towards them.

'Oh Tom,' cried Sophie, desperately, 'you are the clever one, you think of something.'

Tom seized Sophie's hand, the one which was still clutching the frog's leg, 'I will always believe what you tell us,' he shouted, ' and .... and .... and, I'll never harm another spider as long as I live.'

And suddenly, Tom and Sophie found themselves lying, tangled up together, in the bath which, luckily was empty, though the cold water tap was dripping uncomfortably down Tom's neck. He scrambled up and quickly put the plug into the hole and stood upon it for several minutes, until he was sure that MUCH BIGGER BROTHER SPIDER wasn't still following them.

Finally, they both agreed that they were safe, and crept quietly back to their beds where, to their surprise, they slept soundly until morning.

Sophie kept her promise to give her curls to extra-granny. She told her mother that she had grown fed up with ringlets and had cut them off and thrown them away. Her mother was so surprised that Sophie, who had always been so good, had now done something naughty, that she forgot to punish her. Instead, because she thought she must be ill, she sent her to bed for the day, which was just as bad. However, Sophie, who felt rather guilty at not being completely truthful about her ringlets, did not complain.

Tom was much more respectful towards extra-granny and was pleased to find that she became more kindly towards him. He never did harm another spider. He also never again left the plug in when the bath was empty.

'If the little spiders can get into and out of the bath on their own,' he explained to Sophie, 'MUCH BIGGER BROTHER SPIDER will never need to come and help them again.'

Sophie laughed, but agreed.

© 2004 Jim Burch

SCENE FROM THE TRAIN

They looked at first
Like turds,
Dropped so neatly
Down the lines of stubble,
Then like eyebrows,
Each with a corner raised
And pointing,
But they were pheasants,
Soon,
When flushed,
To rise like startled laughter,
Fall like frowns.

© 2004 Jim Burch

WIDE-AWAKE CLAIRE

Claire was a happy young lady, except that she could not sleep. She had a comfortable house, and enough money for food and clothes and other necessities and a few luxuries also, such as books and holidays. Most of her friends, especially those who were less well off, envied her. But, night after night, she would lie awake, too tired to read, but not tired enough to sleep, staring into the darkness, waiting for morning to come. As the sun rose, she always felt better, and able to face another day.

She had taken advice from friends and doctors, and tried many different kinds of medicines, but none seemed to help. She had tried listening to calm, relaxing music. She had tried vigorous exercise, hoping to exhaust herself into sleep but still, as night fell, the familiar, wakeful restlessness returned. To her friends' eyes, it seemed that, as each day passed, she seemed a little less fit, a little less the true, sparkling Claire they had been used to.

One morning, as she sat on her bed, facing a new day, she made a decision. 'I'll travel. It is foolish to pass my whole life worrying, as I do, about sleeping, or rather, not sleeping. I'll go and see the world. Who knows, somewhere I might meet someone who can help me.' And this is what she did.

It turned out that Claire was an excellent traveller. Everywhere she went she quickly made friends, and the friends she made were good friends, people who not only enjoyed her company, and made her feel comfortable in theirs, but who wished to help her, look after her, and protect her. Everywhere too, these new friends had new remedies to offer for her problem. They would listen sympathetically as she told them of it and then say, 'Ah! But have you tried this? This is what, in our family, we always do. It works for us. Why don't you try it?' And she would. She tried sleeping with a carefully folded sheet of brown paper under her pillow. She arranged her bed so that her feet pointed North. She sipped a drink made of lemon juice, honey and cloves. She went to bed in a room lit by a dim, green lamp. In one house her friends gathered round her bed and took turns to tell her soothing stories. In another they sang lullabies. Sometimes the friends would all fall asleep, but never Claire and, in the mornings the friends would apologise and then try hard to think of some other way in which they could help.

'Don't worry,' Claire would say, 'I am so grateful to you for trying, and for being so kind to me. I will always remember you with gratitude. But there are lots of other places for me to visit. In one of them, I am sure, I will be lucky, and find something that works for me.' And she would take leave of her friends and move on to another town, or another country where .... the same things would happen all over again.

For nearly a year she travelled, and in all of the many places she visited in that time she made, and left behind, wonderful friends. Always they were very happy to meet her. Always they tried to help her. But always they failed, and it was with some sorrow that they would see her go.

As time passed however, Claire gradually became ill. Whether this was from her continuing lack of sleep, or from her constant travelling, would be hard to say but, by the end of the year she was clearly unwell and unable to continue.

'I'd better use what strength I have left to get myself home,' she thought, and this is what she did, though only with great difficulty for, by now, she was very weak.

Her friends at home were shocked to see her. Although sometimes, by day, she was able to entertain them by telling of her adventures, when her eyes would sparkle and her voice light up in the way they remembered, for most of the time she was pale and tired and listless. She had become thin, weak and frail so that she had to spend most of her time in bed.

One day she was visited by a favourite uncle. He sat beside her bed, holding one of her hands in his.

'Was I foolish to go travelling uncle?' she asked him. 'Was it that which has destroyed my health?'

'I don't think so,' he replied. 'Things were not a great deal better before you left, and think of all the good times you have had, many more than if you had stayed at home.'

Claire nodded. 'But now I am going to die, aren't I uncle?' she asked him.

'It does look like it my dear,' he replied, squeezing her hand.

'What shall I do?' she asked, too tired even to be upset by his reply.

'I don't know,' he said. 'It is for you to decide. But I do have a suggestion.'

'Tell me,' whispered Claire.

'I think it is time to forget all about this sleeping business,' he said. 'It has been a long battle. You have fought bravely, but.......... it looks as though you have lost.'

A small tear crept from the corner of Claire's eye. Her uncle carefully wiped it away before he continued.

'I suggest that you waste no more of your time fussing about sleeping,' he said. 'I think you should spend whatever time you have left as pleasantly as possible. All these good friends you made in your travels, visit them again.'

'But how can I?' Claire protested.

'Not really visit them, you have already done that. I mean in your thoughts, in your memory, in your imagination. Go back to them, one at a time. Spend more time with them. Remember what you liked about them. Don't hurry away from any of them. Enjoy their company all over again. Please. Close your eyes and try it.'

Claire did as she was asked. She closed her eyes and went on an imaginary journey to Pedro and his family, the first destination on her real travels. Soon, this imagined journey began to seem very real. She remembered playing with their new baby and could hear again his gurgles and his laughter. She remembered walking in their vineyard, listening to their music, joining in their songs. She remembered trying new foods, and her surprise at finding how much she enjoyed them.

As Claire re-visited these scenes and these experiences, her uncle, who remained at her side, still holding her hand, could see that her breathing had become more settled and her features less tense. It was almost as though she had drifted into sleep.

After several hours Claire opened her eyes, to find her uncle still there and still watching her.

'Where have you been little one?' he asked, gently.

'I went to see Pedro, it was lovely,' she said drowsily, as her eyes began to close again.

'Continue your journey,' called her uncle softly.

And so it went on during the rest of the night and into the next day. Claire visited Sven, who made it possible for her to ride on a reindeer, Big Feather, who taught her how to paddle a canoe, Lee Pin, who showed her how to make and cook noodles, Christine, who took her for long walks into snow-covered mountains, and little Carlo, who had come to love Claire so much that he cried and clung to her when it was time for her to leave. One after another she visited all of these distant friends, and who knows whether these were thoughts or dreams, but what is certain is that for the first time for many a year she slept, soundly and sweetly, and each time she woke she looked a little more refreshed and ready for the next stage on her journey.

This was the beginning of Claire's recovery. Sleeping was never, for her, a problem again. Now, each evening, she would look forward to the travels that awaited her during the night, and she was always grateful to her uncle who, perhaps by chance, but certainly from kindness and love, had discovered a way to help her. She was grateful too for her friends who, even whilst fearing that they had failed her, had built for her a path towards being well again.

'Did you know that I would get better?' she asked her uncle one day.

'I thought that you might die,' he replied, 'but if that was to be so, I wanted you to die happy. But I hoped that you would sleep, and live, and then be even happier, and make me happy too.'

'Clever uncle,' said Claire.

'Lucky uncle,' he replied.

© 2004 Jim Burch

SPATIAL PREJUDICE

Chastening really,
After all the rude things
I've said about our local flatlands,
Not fellscape or lakelands,
But grainlands,
Prairie,
With nary a tree
Or hill
That,
Driving again
Out of the lane,
Past that ever-snatching bramble,
Turning towards Barley,
A daily manoeuvre for fifteen years,
There, on the horizon,
High on the horizon,
I see a wooded ridge,
A well-treed headland,
Sticking up,
Conspicuous indeed.

It's the same every day now.
I find on the map
It's a tail-end of Chiltern.
I still can't believe it.

And,
How does one start again
With a once familiar
Now uppity landscape?

Are apologies demanded?
Somehow I'd rather Martians had landed.

© 2004 Jim Burch

SO, WE MOVED TO THIS PLACE, JUST A FEW MILES SHORT OF PARADISE

There is a bus service
But there aren't many buses
And you can't count on them.
There used to be a shop here
But it closed.
The postman used to come early
Before people left for work
But he retired.
The new one comes later.
Their letters seem stale now in the evening
When they get home.
You can't walk much in the country you know.
The cars go quite fast down our road.
There aren't any pavements
And each side of the road there are steep banks.
You couldn't climb them.
Not in a hurry.
No street lamps either
And away from the street
Only the two same walks.
Down the edge of the field
Or over the road and the stiles and the heavy wobbly gate
And bits of spiky wire
And past the sheep.
The septic tank can be a nuisance.
In summer it smells.
The locals are funny too.
In the pub
They just look at you sometimes
Dad says.
You say, 'Good evening',
They say nothing.
One or two are nice though.
There's one picks me up in his car.
Takes me to the chiropodist.

The people there talk.
Old people mainly.
I can't see them properly now
But they remember me from the shop.
There's a windmill down the road.
Visitors like it.
The church is all right I suppose.
We don't go there.
We went on one of their outings.
The vicar got drunk.

Pity we're on a hill really.
It was flatter in London
And there were shops
And more buses.
More places to go
And not so much mud.
When I was younger
I didn't mind hills.
I used to push the pram
With young Billy in it
Right up to Eltham Church
Then all the way up the High Street
Then home again
With all of the shopping
And six or eight library books.
Everywhere's too far to walk now.
I have to sit down.
We don't get many people calling,
Just a few Jehovah's Witnesses or Christian Scientists or Mormons.
I usually say, 'Sorry,'
And shut the door before they've said much.
I expect they get used to it.
I always wanted to live in the country.

© 2004 Jim Burch

THE RATTLING LAD

Tom couldn't tell when it started, but it had been happening as far back as he could remember. His mother would say that he had always been difficult, even as a baby, and his father agreed. Tom's problem was that he rattled, and his rattling got on people's nerves. Then they would complain, and this got on Tom's nerves. And when Tom's nerves were bad, he rattled even more.

When a doctor explained this to Tom's mother, she refused to accept it. 'Nonsense! He's too young to have nerves,' she said. But, it wasn't nonsense. It was true.

Luckily, it was also true that, if people were nice to Tom, he did not rattle nearly so much. 'When people are nice,' thought Tom, 'its as though I fill up with honey or golden syrup, like when dad puts oil in his car. The rattling isn't nearly so bad.'

The doctor explained this to Tom's mother too. 'Humph!' she said, 'spoil him you mean!' 'No, just love him,' said the doctor. 'Love him indeed,' Tom's mum replied, twitching her shoulders closer to her body as though she feared they were coming loose.

In fact, she did love Tom very much, in spite of often being very angry with him, but, for some reason, it was not something she liked talking about. When people talked about love Tom's mum would accuse them of being soft or soppy and would get up and rattle some pots and pans, as though she had too much work to do to sit around talking nonsense. Tom sometimes wondered whether he had caught his rattling from his mother's pots and pans.

Tom found it hard to describe his rattling, even to himself. He could never be sure whether it came from inside his body, or whether it came from his bumping into things. Certainly, things did seem to move about, squeak, rattle, clatter, shake, fall and break whenever Tom was about. Especially if he was in one of what people called 'his moods.'

If he sat on a chair, it immediately began to move about, squeaking as it scraped on the floor, or banging if it bumped against a table or a desk. Sometimes Tom would slide off the chair and finish up on the floor. Or Tom and the chair would both fall over with a loud crash which, Tom's mother would exclaim, would one day make her, 'Jump out of my skin.'

Animals did not seem to be bothered by him and would lick his hands, nuzzle up close to him and follow him if he went for a walk. But people, even strangers, would tend to move away, as though they thought that Tom might suddenly explode.

When he undressed to go to bed, his clothes would be all over the place. One sock would be in a corner, another under the bed, one shoe upstairs, the other down, his shirt in the bathroom, his trousers in the toy cupboard. His father insisted that once, he found Tom's jumper in the 'fridge and his mother would exclaim that she was quite sure that one day, she would return home to find Tom himself, in bits and pieces, scattered all over the house, just like his clothes. 'You'll rattle yourself to pieces,' she would say.

At first, when he was small, Tom used to get quite upset when he heard this, and cry a few rattly tears. Then, his Mum would pull him onto her lap and wrap her arms tightly around him and say,'Now you are safe, now you won't fall to pieces, will you?' And she'd count his arms and legs, and his fingers and toes, and his eyes and ears, and his ankles and knees just to make sure that he was, 'All present and correct.' Sometimes she would look under her chair to see whether any bits had fallen off and would pretend to find his nose there and polish it carefully on her handkerchief before fixing it back on. Then Tom would feel really sure that all his bits and pieces were back together again, oiled and soothed with golden syrup, and not rattling at all.

Later, when Tom felt that he was too old to cry, and his mother felt that he was too big and heavy to put on her lap, she'd hold his hand instead, or ruffle his hair, and her voice would change, and he'd still get what he called his 'treacly feeling', and his rattling would die down.

In school, it was worst in quiet times, when everyone was supposed to be sitting still. The headmaster used to complain that, at assemblies, Tom was like 'a one-boy Mexican wave.' When children were lining up for school dinners, or to leave the hall, Tom always seemed to have his head sticking out one side of the line, and his arms and legs sticking out the other. In painting lessons Tom always got more paint on his face and hands and clothes, than he did on his paper.

It seemed to Tom that the only thing he was good at was 'Playing'. But he was also good at games and singing. If his school work was difficult or boring, then Tom's rattling became very loud indeed. But, if it was interesting and he could do it, then he could work much more quietly. 'Aha!' his teacher would say, 'Tom is humming along nicely today.'

When, after he had left school, Tom met Jenny, the girl he was going to marry, he became very nervous and rattly indeed. But, once they were married, the rattling stopped, except when they had an argument, which was not very often. If Tom came home, rattling a bit from troubles at work, then, pretty soon, in his own home and with Jenny, the rattling would calm down and stop. 'Its honey and treacle every day now,' he would think.

Most of his life, this rattling business had been a problem for Tom. It bothered other people and then they bothered him. But, in the end, he came to accept it, and would say things like, 'I think everybody has a few rattlings in their life, even if other people can't aways hear them. Its how you cope with them that counts.'

When his own son got rattled from time to time, Tom found that he was quick to notice this, and he would take the boy for a walk, or play a game with him in the garden, or sit with him and tell him a story, or, lift him up and put him onto his mother's or grand-mother's lap. That always seemed to work. 'Treacle time,' is what he called it.

© 2004 Jim Burch

DANIEL'S DREAM

Daniel lived with his mother, at the edge of a village, beside a river and near to a forest. His father used to work in the forest, before he fell ill and died.

After the burial, Daniel asked his mother what would happen to his father now.' I'm not sure Daniel,' she said, 'but there is an old story that, for a while, he will lie peacefully in the earth. Then, later, his body will gradually change, into small, very small pieces, and the pieces will go into the ground, into the grass, into the flowers and the trees, into the river and the clouds.'

Daniel thought about this one day as he was walking in the woods. He looked hard at a tree. It looked strong and tall, just as his father was before he became ill. He looked again, and saw that it was just a tree, and he walked on.

He laid down on some grass which had just been cut and felt the rough, short stems scratching against his cheek. It reminded him of his father's chin, when he had not shaved, and it pressed against Daniel's face as he sat on his father's lap to hear a story. He lay there for a time, with his eyes closed, feeling the rough grass and thinking of his father and his stories. Then he opened his eyes and looked hard at the ground in front of him, but all he could see was grass.

He rolled over onto his back and looked up at the sky and, for a moment, one of the clouds looked just like his father's face looking down at him. And then it was just a cloud.

When he saw the spade, propped against the tree, near where they grew their vegetables, it looked as though it was waiting for a hand to seize it and dig it firmly into the earth, just as his father used to do. But then it was just a spade. He picked it up and put it away in the shed with the other tools.

He went to the river, watching closely as it splashed quickly past. As he looked at the rocks, which all the villagers used as stepping stones to cross the river, he thought for a moment that he could see his father's feet, skipping from one rock to the next, as they used to when he ran, laughing, across to the other side. Then he looked again, and there was just the river, and the rocks.

When he got home his mother asked him where he had been. 'I've been looking for my dad,' he said, in a puzzled voice. His mother said nothing for a while, then asked, in her quietest voice, 'and what did you find?'

'You said he would go into the ground, and the grass, and the trees, and the river, and the clouds, so I went to look. I wanted to see him again.'

'And what did you find?' she asked again, sitting beside him.

'I kept thinking I could see him........in that big tree by the forest path, and in the grass, and in the clouds and the river, and in the garden where he used to dig, but....'

'But what?' asked his mother.

'But, like you said, it was only little bits of him. It was only little, little bits of Dad....I couldn't see him properly.'

His mother pulled him against her and rested her cheek against his hair. 'Where do you see him, or hear him best Daniel?' she asked.

'When I just think about him,' said Daniel. 'When I'm here and quiet and thinking about him, or when I am dreaming. Especially when I am dreaming. Then he seems altogether again, the way he was.'

'I see him too, Daniel,' said his mother, 'and I think I can now tell you the end of the story.' Daniel knew which story she was talking about. 'The story says that after the body has rested, it is then scattered all around the world, in the soil, the rain, the plants, the clouds, everywhere, in tiny drops, all around, everywhere in the world. But then, they begin to feel tired, and lonely. They want to join up again, to come together again, to rest and be comfortable. And they think, 'Where, in all the world, is the best place for us to be? Where will we be loved? Where will we be remembered?' And with daddy we know now that he has chosen here and here,' and she touched herself just above her heart and on her head, 'and here and here,' and now she lightly touched Daniel just above his heart and upon his head.

Daniel thought of his dead father, buried in the ground, then scattered around the world and then coming back to rest where he would be remembered and loved by his wife and his son. And Daniel kept and cherished the memory of his father, like a precious cargo, for the rest of his life.

© 2004 Jim Burch

LITTLE DOLPHIN

Little Dolphin wanted to be friendly, but it is difficult to be friendly when you spend most of your time on your own. He had heard of dolphins who had rescued people from drowning but, though he often followed boats of all shapes and sizes, no-one ever fell overboard, so his chance to rescue them never came. He had also heard of faraway dolphins who entertained great crowds of people by jumping through hoops, but there did not seem to be any hoops to jump through in his part of the ocean.

One day, in one of his favourite spots, where there was a small beach, surrounded by cliffs, and where, above the cliffs, the green, grass sloped upwards towards a few houses and a small church with little white stones sticking up out of the ground around it, he noticed a small figure standing near the edge of the cliff. From the way the wind blew her hair and her clothes, he could see that it was a little girl. She waved, and in reply he gave a little leap taking his body gracefully out of the water and then back in again with scarcely a splash.

She waved again, and he gave another jump. Then she waved with both hands, holding them high in the air, and gave little, excited jumps. Little Dolphin sank lower into the water and then, with a twist of his body and a flip from his tail, swam rapidly upwards, breaking through the surface and rising high into the air, this time landing with a deliberately huge splash. As he rose again, his head poking gently above the waves, the water streaming away from his eyes, he could see the little girl skipping and dancing about in a circle, waving both of her hands, then clapping them together, until she turned and went back up the slope of the hill to one of the houses.

Little Dolphin returned the next day, and there was more waving and jumping, and skipping and splashing. And the little girl and Little Dolphin enjoyed each other's company in this way for many weeks. Some days the little girl's mother would come with her, and both of them would wave. Then it seemed that the mother came every day. Though they both still waved to Little Dolphin, and he still gave his biggest jumps and loudest splashes, the little girl no longer jumped up and down, or ran about, or skipped in a circle as she used to do. Then, one day, and for many days more, neither the little girl or her mother came at all.

Day after day Little Dolphin returned to the same spot, but the cliffs were empty. Each day his head pushed a little more slowly out of the sea, and each day the water seemed to take a little longer to clear from his eyes, but though he waited and waited, there was no sign of the little girl.

Just as he was beginning to believe that he would never see her again, just as he was pushing his head sadly through the surface of the sea, and waiting for the water to clear from his eyes, he did see something, up there, at the edge of the cliff. It was the mother, and beside her a sort of chair, with big wheels at the side. On the chair, someone was sitting, but at first he couldn't see who. But then, as he bobbed his head a little higher to get a better look, the figure in the chair gave that familiar wave, first with one hand, then with two. The hands which waved to him looked tired, but they told him that, 'Yes!' this was the little girl. She had come back.

Little Dolphin dove down deep into the sea, and then came up with a rush to make one of the highest jumps he had ever done, and come down with the biggest splash ever. He then did three more leaps and splashes before he stopped to float again, with his head just out of the water. The little girl and her mother were still there, and they gave a few more waves, before going back up the slope, the mother pushing the chair with wheels in front of her.

Little Dolphin was very happy to see the little girl again. But he was puzzled, and a little bit sad that she now sat down all the time, that she didn't stand up, or run, or skip about, or jump up in the air as she used to. What the little girl's parent's knew, and the other people in the village knew as well, was that the little girl was very ill indeed. They were sad to see the little girl, who had been so cheerful and full of energy, now so tired and pale and wondered what they could do to bring more happiness into her life.

Knowing how much she enjoyed watching Little Dolphin doing his jumps, they began collecting money to pay for a trip to that far off place they had heard of where there were lots of dolphins, who jumped through hoops, and could jump and take a fish from a man's hand. But the doctor said that the little girl was too ill to travel so far, and the mother said that it might make her unhappy to see dolphins kept away from the sea. She was sure that her daughter would prefer to go on watching her very own Little Dolphin, who had the whole sea to swim in, but freely chose to come each day to see the little girl.

Then one of the villagers had another idea, and the mother agreed that this idea was a much better one. Using the money they had collected, and with everyone helping as best they could, they built a kind of lift. It was like a cage, which could be lowered down the cliff to the beach below, and from that point they built a path that went right down to the very edge of the sea. After they had tested it to make quite sure that it was safe, the little girl and her parents went into the lift, which was then gently lowered down the cliff. The little girl was nervous, but also very excited.

Next, the parents pushed the wheelchair along the path until they reached the water. The tide was in, so the last part of the path was covered. Carefully they went further, until the water was halfway up the wheels. Then they waited. But not for long.

Little Dolphin, who had been watching from afar with a great deal of interest, suddenly popped his head out of the water just a few feet away from them. The little girl bounced in her seat with joy, and stretched out a hand towards him. With his eyes fixed upon her, Little Dolphin tried to come closer, but the water was not deep enough for him to do so. The two gazed lovingly but sadly at each other until the father picked his daughter up, and walked out into the sea until the water came up to his chest.

Little Dolphin was now very close, and then moved closer. The little girl could now reach him with her outstretched hand, and she stroked his head, and talked to him. Once, Little Dolphin was able to come close enough to brush her cheek gently with his snout. To the little girl it was as though he was kissing her.

They heard shouts from the top of the cliffs. The villagers had stayed there, afraid that a crowd of them on the beach might frighten Little Dolphin away, but they could see all that happened and were cheering because their plan had been so successful.

'Time to get home, and into some warm, dry clothes,' said the father, and the family set off back along the path, onto the lift, and up to the top of the cliff. The villagers cheered again, and the little girl and her parents thanked all of their friends for their wonderful gift. As Little Dolphin watched, they gave a few more waves from their usual spot on the cliffs, and then went up the hill towards home.

For a while, the little girl came down to the beach every day, and every time, she would insist that one of her parents should carry her far enough into the sea for her to be able to stroke the head of Little Dolphin. These were very happy days for both of them. But it seemed to the dolphin that every day, his little friend's hands felt weaker and weaker as they tenderly stroked his head.

Then came a day when the little girl and her mother stayed at the top of the cliff, as before, instead of coming down to the beach. They waved to him and he gave several of his highest jumps, but, after a short while, they returned home. The same happened the next day, and the next, but after that, no-one came and, even though Little Dolphin returned to the same spot every day, there was no sign of the little girl or her parents.

A few days later, as Little Dolphin watched and waited, he saw a line of people coming down the hill from the village, towards the cliff edge. At the front of the line were the father and mother, and they were pushing the chair with wheels. But there was no sign of the little girl. Instead, on the chair, was a small white box with some flowers, and there were two other people, one walking each side of the chair, to hold the box and the flowers steady.

When they reached the spot where the little girl used to stand, all of the people stopped, and lined up along the edge of the cliff and waved to Little Dolphin. He gave a couple of small jumps, and two small splashes, but mainly he was looking for any sign of the little girl. After a while, the people walked back up the hill towards the church, and as they did so, the church bell began to ring slowly, just one sad note, 'Dong, dong, dong, dong.' The people went into the church and, after a while, came out again, and gathered in the place where there were small white stones. Then they all went home, the parents still pushing the wheelchair, but without the little, white box.

Day after day Little Dolphin returned, and day after day it seemed to him that, as he pushed his head out of the water to search the cliff for the little girl, the water took longer to clear from his eyes. Sometimes the mother, or the father, would come to wave to him, but never the little girl.

However, all of the villagers now loved him too, and many of them would wave to him from the cliff-top, as they saw him bobbing and waiting out at sea. Also, the lift and the path, built for the little girl, now made it easier for people to come to the beach, and many of them did. Sometimes, if there were small children, Little Dolphin would come very close and allow himself to be stroked, just as the little girl used to stroke him.

Another thing, the story of the great friendship between Little Dolphin and the little girl had spread far and wide. People from other villages and further towns, and even foreign countries, would visit the spot on the cliffs to wave to Little Dolphin, or go down to the beach in the hope of being allowed to stroke his head. So Little Dolphin now had many new friends. But a greater joy was yet to come.

One day, the mother said to the father, 'We collected money so that our little girl could see Little Dolphin. Let us now make another collection so that Little Dolphin can still see our little girl.' Then she explained what she meant.

Many weeks later, as Little Dolphin looked towards the cliff-tops, he saw a big crowd of people gathered there, and in their midst was something covered by a big white sheet. Then all the people turned towards him and waved and, as they did so, the sheet fell to the ground to reveal his little girl, standing as she always used to, with an arm raised to wave to him.

Little Dolphin gave ten great leaps, and ten great splashes, before he looked again. They were all still there. Finally with a last wave, and a loud cheer, the people turned and walked slowly back up the hill. But the little girl remained, on the same spot, and with her hand still held high.

People on passing ships would see the little girl and, though it was only a statue, it was so life-like, that nearly always they found themselves waving back to her. But Little Dolphin knew that the little waving hand was meant only for him.

© 2004 Jim Burch

CHRIS GUTTERIDGE

Chris Gutteridge is a website designer and musician, playing such obscure instruments as the serpent and the lysard with his bands, "The King's Lynn Waites" and "The Fall of Eve". He has been a member of King's Lynn Writers' Circle for about ten years, and Chairman for the past six. He has always had an interest in writing, and after several attempts at novels, settled to short stories and poems. His stories, articles and poems have been published in numerous magazines and anthologies, and his own anthology of his poems, "An English Man At Home" (ISBN 0 9535822 0 5), was published in 1999.

IRSTEAD SHOALS

Birches cast gold sovereigns in our path
As we glide silently over green glass
Escorted by a flashing blue kingfisher.

The world is at peace. Sleeping
Anglers, nodding at their rods,
Stir as our quant grates on gravel.

We emerge into September sunlight,
Sails flapping and filling
With the breeze off the reedbed.

© 2004 Chris Gutteridge

WE GOT ONE O' THEM FEMERNISTS MOVED IN NEXT DOOR

I din't realise tha's what she were at first, mind. She got a little ol' boy, he hint more'n knee high ter a grasshopper, so I s'pose that hint that long since she saw suffin' in one man at least, but she hint got no time for none on us nowadays.

I was in the back place th'other day, when I heard a haltercation down the garden. That was her next door an my missus an they was a'goin hammer n'tongs. Her next door, she's a-shriekun an' a-hollerin an' a-goin' ahid.

"I can't believe I'm a-hearin' this!" she say. I think, what's that she's a-hearin'? An' I push th'ol winder open a bit so's I can find out.

That turn out my ol' missus is stickin' up for us men. I must say I couldn't quite believe that myself! An' she wasn't shoutin'. She was as cool as a cucumber, but she stood her ground. She say tha's all very well runnin down men in general, but she hint got no complaints an' if her next door go an' pick a wrong 'un she hint got no call to go a-tarrin' em all wi' the same brush.

One thing I din't like the sound of. Her next door she say she got so fed up wi' her ol' man, she stabbed him wi' th'kitchern knife. Well, I had bin thinkin' a offerin' ter help her with her garden an' that when she first move in, seein' as how she was single-like. I'm glad I din't now. Them garden himplements is worse'n kitchern knives.

Anyhow, my ol' girl she have the last word, an' I hear next door's back door slam.

When my missus come in I was all ready to say suffin' to her, I was suffin' proud o' the way she stuck up for me, but she say "What you standin' there a-grinnin' all over yer ugly ol' face for? Have you finished th'washin' up yet?"

So I just dried the knives an' put un away in the draw quiet, like.

© 2004 Chris Gutteridge

STREAM OF CONSCIOUSNESS

Why does this tiny trickle mean so much to me –
Rebellious upsurge where it shouldn't be?
Each time I turn the corner hoping that it's there,
Running down the road to meet me.

A little glimpse of Wales upon a Norfolk hill –
A tiny brief reminder of a Lakeland rill.
The sheepish bleating of shy Brian's pets
Sometimes contributes to the spell.

But more than this it seems to represent to me
My own rebelliousness against conformity.
For what harm's in a little water on the road
Save that it's where it shouldn't be?

They come with yellow jackets in a yellow van
To subdue this wisp of water to the will of man,
Thrusting it underground with rods of cane.
They've hardly gone before it's back again.

© 2004 Chris Gutteridge

I BIKE UP TOWN MOST TUESDIES

Least, I dun't bike much these days. Me an' th'ol' bike, we come to an agreement. I ride down the hills, an' we lean on each other goin' up. Tha's a good ol' bike but that seem t'have got heavier just lately. Tha's one o' them trade bikes wi' a ol' orange box on th' front t'put yer bits o' things in. When I had a little ol' dog, he used ter sit in th'box, good as gold. He was a good ol' dog.

Anyhow, what I was a-leadin' up to was, I was pushin' th'ol bike up th'hill past the horspital last Tuesdie when our young Darren come past on one o' them new mounting bikes. He slow right down an' ride alongside o' me, an' he say, "I don't know what you heve a bike for, Grandad. I hint never sin you ridin' it."

I just kep' ploddin' on. He can be a cheeky ol' boy, but I don't mind him. Then he say, "What you need is one o' these here mounting bikes like I're got. You hint got no gears, have yer."

Well, my ol' missus have got a Sturmey-Archer three-speed on her bike, but that's a ladies bike. She don't get that out much, but do she do she don't use the gears. She say they're an added comperlication.

Well, young Darren, he start ridin' round an' round me on his mounting bike 'till that fare make my head spin; an he kep a-clickin' an' a-clatterin' them ol' gears. He say, "I got twenty-five gears, so I can ride anywhere. You kin even ride up mountins on a bike like this."

I say, "That must be very useful round here." He din't say nothin'. He just kep' on goin' around an' around, so I say, "won't that go in a straight line, then?" He shot off up the road and I didn't see him no more.

© 2004 Chris Gutteridge

ACLE BRIDGE TO THURNE MOUTH

Surging through wide golden Bure,
alone with the autumn sunset,
I gaze down from cabin roof
At our foaming prow.

Running against rolling tide,
our bow wave, increased
by my forward weight,
splashes the foredeck.

Remembering,
I feel the slippery-smooth mast in my palm
And wish I was there.

© 2004 Chris Gutteridge

OUR YOUNG DARREN, HE'S ON THE HINTERNET

We was round theirs th'other night, an he say come'n' look what I got Grandad. He take me in the spare room an' sit me down in front o' this here telly, only that hint a proper telly.

He say, "Now come on, Grandad, what're you hinterested in?"

I say, "I wouldn't mind a pint o' beer." He type in beer or suffin' like that on his keyboard thing, an' all these words come on th'telly. I din't have me glasses so I couldn't tell yer what that said, 'xactly.

"Now what's your favourite beer, Grandad?" he say.

"You know as well as me," I say. "I like a pint of Adamson's, brewed in Norfolk, same as my ol' Daddy useter drink."

So he type in Adamson's. Suddenly th'ol' telly screen say "Welcome to th' Website o' Multi-Conglomerate Breweries Hinternational" in great big letters.

I say "Who're they when they're at home?"

Darren, he say, "They make Adamson's, Grandad, din't you know that?"

I say, "No, I din't, an' I din't want to. Where's my beer?" I was thinkin' he'd have a job gettin' a pint o' beer out on the telly, whatever that say on th'screen.

He say, "Hold on, I'll print you off all about Adamson's," an' he press some buttons an' this ol' machine in the corner start up.

"You keep an eye on that, Grandad," he say, "I just got to go an' download," an' he head off for the smallest room.

Well I sat an watched that ol' machine a-clatterin' an' a hummin' in th' corner, an' that kep' on a-spoutin' out paper 'till that was all over the floor.

When he come back he got in a right ol' stew. He say, "I thought you was a-watchin' it for me."

I say, "I din't take me eyes off on it."

I never did get my beer. Mind you, Adamson's don't seem to taste the same since then, I don't know why.

© 2004 Chris Gutteridge

LEZIATE

Its name means gate to the lees,
It has views and beautiful trees,
But Leziate stands
On some very fine sands,
Full of holes, like a piece of Swiss cheese.

© 2004 Chris Gutteridge

WE GOT NEW NEIGHBOURS AGIN

No, not the femernist – she's still there, though we don't see her out the back much since her and my missus had words. That's the other side, now. Old Mrs Spinks, she upped and died a month or two back, and her family have sold her little old place.

I was on the garden th'other day, and this young fella, he look over the fence and he say, "Hi," he say. That's them Americans done that. That's not the only thing they left ahind after they was over here – nor that hint the worst, neither!

Anyways, he say "Hi, I'm Toby, your new neighbour", and he put his hand out for to shake hands. Well, that put me at a bit of a stand. I didn't want to appear unfriendly, so I wipe me hand on me corduroys, and I go over.

That's a funny thing, but I didn't know rightly what to call myself. Mr Balls sound a bit formal, and not many people use my first name. My Mrs call me all sorts a things, and my mates have called me Michael since I was a little totty old boy, but that hint my right name. Most people can't remember why I got called that, and I hint in no hurry to remind them, but that's another story.

So, anyway, I take his hand, and I say, "Pleased to meet you, my name's Alfred."

There's a young lady stand next ter him, and he say, "This is my partner, Alex."

So I say, "What line of business are you in, then," just making conversation.

They look at me gone out, then he laugh and say, "No, Alex is my significant other".

"Other than what," I say, and I feel I'm loosing the thread.

Then she smile at me, an that's a nice smile, when she bother ter use it, an she say, "Toby and me live together." Well, I didn't know where to put myself. That don't bother me what other folks git up to, and I know that's the way these youngsters are, now, but I felt a bit of a fool, not catching on.

Anyway, the Mrs then call me in for my docky, so I bid them good day.

Well, I had my bit of bread and cheese, and a cup of coffee, and I told the Mrs all about it. Of course, that turn out she know more than me already.

"That's their second home," she say.

"Where'd they used to live, then?" I ask.

"No, you silly old fool, I mean they got another home, in London, where they work. This here's only their home for weekends and holidays. As a matter of fact," she say, "They asked me round yesterday while you was up town. I forgot to mention it. They give me a key in case there's any trouble when they're not here. And I'll tell you something else, and all. They had their wedding photo on top of the telly."

"So what do they want to go telling me they're living together for, then?"

"Well, I suppose they are, in a manner of speaking. I reckon that's got now so as young folk are ashamed to say they're decently married."

I took the cups through to the back place to rinse them, and then I had a thought. I put my head round the door, and I say, "Well, my dear, that look as if that make you my significant other!"

"I'll show you what's significant, you silly old bugger!" she say, "Hint you got nothing useful you can be doing?"

© 2004 Chris Gutteridge

SHAKESPEAREAN LIMERICK

Compared with the best Summer's day
You're better in every way:
Less windy, consistent
And far more persistent.
This verse means that you're here to stay.

LEARIAN SONNET

Oh, aged, bearded sir, your fears are just.
Your facial follicles have been invaded.
Alas, the British Ornithological Trust
And RSPB cannot be evaded.
You must admit, to have a nesting hen
So close to where your breakfast goes is handy,
And larks are cheery creatures, but the wren
Is fierce, aggressive and, I've heard, quite randy:
And owls, though beautiful, are still nocturnal
And feed their young on rats and other vermin –
The noise and smell from them must be infernal.
So here I fear is what you must determine:
Shave, and break the law: or do your duty –
Declare your beard an Area of Natural Beauty.

© 2004 Chris Gutteridge

HAVE YOU HEARD ABOUT OUR NEW RECTOR?

Well, you know since old Mr Hardisty retired we been havin' a hinter-rectum; though why vicars retire these days I don't know. They never used to, did they? They used to go on till they dropped, didn't they? These days though, they want decent wages 'n' pension plans an' all sorts. That hint right, is it?

Still, tha's all beside the point. We come to the end o' our hinter-rectum at last, an' we got a new rector, but you'll never guess what! No, that hint one o' them women priests, least not 'xacly. I couldn't be havin' none o' that nonsense. I hint goin' to Chuch a-Sunday to be preached at by some old mawther. I can git that at home any day o' the week.

No, tha's suffin different to that. We got a young feller from London. He had one of they inner city parishes, poor feller, an' now they sent him to us for a bit o' peace and quiet, I reckon. But he hint been gettin' it. Trouble is, he's a nice enough old boy, but that turn out he's gay.

That don't bother me. I reckon I hint got much to worry about on that score. An' all the old mawthers, they think the world on him. He's everso neat and partic'lar, an' he 'preciate all they do to trickerlate th'old Chuch up an' that, an' they say he make a lovely cup o' coffee do they drop in round the rectory. He's makin' th'ol' place look real homely, runnin' up the curtains an' that hisself.

No, tha's th'ol' squire wa's got all hot under the collar about it. He say nobody tol' him that was a gay rector till that was too late. He say he hint bein' rector's warden to no shirt-lifter, he say, an' he wrote to the bishop 'n' complained.

The bishop he wrote straight back, and now th'old squire's in a right stew. The bishop he say our rector's a fine man and a good Christian, an' so long as he hint a practisin' howmer sexshuwal that hint nobody's business 'cept his own.

So that seem as if so long as the rector's got the hang o' this here howmer sexshuwal business, tha's alright. Tha's a rumm'n, hint it?

© 2004 Chris Gutteridge

SAILING

The companionable silences,
the unity of thought.
Conversations with others as we drift by.
The werry skipper pausing from bawling out his crew
to pass the time of day with us.

The wild, lonely beauty of early morning and dusk,
with the river to ourselves.
Lying awake listening to the small reed rustlings and splashings
and comfortable squeaks and quacks of waterfowl.
Peering through the porthole at stars reflected on the river.

The exhilaration of surging with straining sails,
across a wide expanse of empty broad,
hanging on grimly to tiller and sheet,
feet braced against the opposite seat.

Even the panic of shooting bridges,
the bungled landfalls and departures,
the mast jamming halfway,
the unforeseen embarrassments,
the post-disaster analysis.

The plotting and planning
and muttered conferences
resulting in smartly executed manoeuvres.
The satisfaction of sails well stowed or set,
of neatly coiled ropes and everything in its place.

© 2004 Chris Gutteridge

ETERNAL TRIANGLE

I don't think I'd ever
Say Pythagoras was clever.
The square on the hypotenuse
Don't seem a lot of use.

PRINCIPLE

Archimedes was Greek – they don't come Greeker –
But he wasn't much of a public speaker.
All he did was shout 'Eureka!'
He made up for it by being a streaker.

ELEVATING

Archimedes' wife said 'You didn't oughta
Go out and leave the bath full of water.'
Archimedes, still naked, said 'What should I do?
I know my dear – I'll give you a screw!'

DISCOVERY

An apple fell on Newton's head
As he sat musing 'neath the tree.
"That's it!" he cried (or so 'tis said)
"I think I'll call it gravity!"

© 2004 Chris Gutteridge

THE WISHING STONE

The sea stretched out in front of Michael in a sullen, grey, oily sheet. With monotonous regularity it flopped a half-hearted wave at his feet and tried to haul itself up the shelving beach, lost its grip and slipped, with a hiss and rattle of shingle, back into itself.

An ominous feeling of expectancy hung in the still, heavy, humid air, making it difficult to breath.

Michael squatted on his haunches. His left hand searched on the beach beside him for flat stones, whilst with the other he flicked the stones into the sea. Each one disappeared at once with a loud plop. It wasn't fair, he thought. Other boys could do it, time after time, and he'd never done it once.

He tried again. Plop. Again. Plop. His left hand passed another stone to his right, groped, felt a smooth, oval, flat stone.

"Wish I could make it skip, just a bit!" he thought. The stone left his hand and skidded over the water, touching the surface once – twice – then dived in.

He stood up. "Cor!" he said aloud. He was about to throw the stone in his hand, but looked down at it. It was pink, translucent, with thin white veins running through it.

"Too pretty to throw," he thought, and keeping it in his left hand he stooped and picked another. Like the first, it skipped twice, then sank. He tried again and again, keeping the pretty pink stone in his left hand, and every one skipped twice then sank.

"Wish I could get one to go on for ever and ever!" he thought, already unimpressed by his new-found skill. The stone he was about to throw seemed to leave his hand of its own volition, and shot off almost parallel to the heaving surface of the ocean. It dipped, lightly touched the surface, rose, dipped again, and again, on and on, until his dazzled eyes lost sight of it. He stood dumbfounded.

"Again!" he shouted, and threw another. It skipped off out of sight. Another. The same. And again, and again, faster and faster, until the surface of the sea seemed covered with skipping stones.

Without thinking he threw the pink stone that had been in his left hand all this time. It plopped into the sea at his feet, and as the wave receded it lay glistening and sparkling on the edge of the water. He bent and picked it up again.

It seemed to have become even hotter and more humid. A storm was brewing. Michael's teeshirt clung uncomfortably to his salty back. "Wish it wasn't so hot!" he thought. At once a breeze sprang up from behind him, ruffling his blond curls. He looked down at the stone in his hand, and a mad, wild thought came into his head.

He looked around him for something to try out his startling theory on. Further along the beach and higher up, his sister Jill was walking slowly along the tideline, scanning the flotsam and jetsam for anything worthwhile. That was all she ever seemed to do on the beach. She usually found something. Once, she found four pound coins, and Dad had let her keep them. She had all the luck, and she always got her own way, because she was older – nearly ten – and a girl. It wasn't fair.

"I wish she'd just disappear," Michael said quietly and deliberately. Then he gave a little, gasping cry. His sister had vanished. The stone dropped from his hand, and just as suddenly she reappeared. He stooped and picked it up. "Again!" he said, and she was gone. He stood and stared at the spot where she had been. Perhaps she had just bent down out of sight to pick something up? He waited for what seemed an age. She didn't come back. He began to feel frightened. What would Dad say? Even worse, what would Mum say? "Didn't mean it!" he burst out, and there was his sister, unconcerned, walking slowly away from him as before.

Michael sat down on the shingle beach and looked at the pink stone in his hand, then he thought very hard. What did he want more than anything else in the world? Loads of money! No. How could he have not thought of it before? He looked up to where his father sat alone, dozing under the sea wall, then, gripping the stone very hard in his left hand, he closed his eyes tight and wished.

"Please, please, please, magic stone," he begged, "Get Mum and Dad back together!" He waited, not daring to open his eyes. Perhaps it wouldn't work straight away, anyhow. Mum was back at home. Perhaps, when Dad took them home, she'd come out to meet him, smiling like she used to, and they'd all go inside together. Just because she wasn't there when he opened his eyes, didn't mean it hadn't worked!

He opened his eyes slightly, and peeped towards his father. Dad was standing up now, and somebody else was standing beside him. They moved close together. It had worked! Dad turned towards him and beckoned. With a cry of "Mum! Dad!" he scrambled to his feet and pounded up the beach, head down, his feet slipping and sliding on the shingle.

As he came up to where his father stood, there was a rumble of distant thunder.

"Time to go, son!"

Michael looked around him. Dad and Jill stood looking at him. There was no sign of Mum. He felt a sickening jolt in his stomach, and looked down at his left hand. It was empty.

"My stone!" he screamed in horror.

Hot tears ran down his cheeks as he broke into racking sobs. Jill rolled her eyes upwards in mocking contempt. Michael looked back across the yards and yards of shingle he had traversed. It was hopeless, but he must try.

"Wait!" he shouted, and started running back, scanning the ground with eyes blurred by tears.

His father ran after him and picked him up.

"Come on, Michael. I've got to get you back to your Mum on time, or she'll start making trouble about me seeing you."

"But...." Michael began. But what was the use? They'd never believe him. Jill would sneer at him. And even if they searched the beach, and against all probability found the stone, it would be Jill who found it. She always did have all the luck. And then it would be Jill's stone, and what would she wish for?

The car pulled up outside the gate. The storm had arrived, and warm rain was lashing down on the windscreen. The front door opened, and Michael could see his mother waiting in the shadows of the hall, but she didn't come out. His father turned and looked at him, sitting alone in the back seat.

"I can't hand you over looking like that, son. Jill, have you got a tissue to clean him up a bit?"

His sister flicked a packet of tissues over her shoulder at him. "Wipe your nose, snot-face!" she said.

© 2004 Chris Gutteridge

GINA GUTTERIDGE

Shakespeare and Tall Ships feature prominently in the life of Gina Gutteridge, the former from the age of fourteen and the latter, as a result of a more recent two week cruise in the Baltic. Gina has always had a passion for reading, writing and the theatre and all found eventual fulfillment when she went in for journalism in 1985. She studied for a degree in 1996 and now works for Norfolk County Council's Adult Education Department teaching English, Creative Writing and Journalism. Gina and her husband, Chris, moved to West Norfolk from Sussex in 1972 and have two grown-up daughters.

MY MOTHER

If, in the early days of the Second World War, a tall, slim, blonde, with an alluring Greta Garbo smile, had not popped into a pub in North Wales to buy some cigarettes, and put her Cocker spaniel puppy on the counter while she rummaged in her handbag for her purse, I would definitely not be here today.

In fact, I undoubtedly owe my existence to this puppy, whose name was Sammy. For Sammy, with the cheek, charm and curiosity of all such pups, wobbled along the bar and drank the beer of a handsome, dark haired army officer, who was deep in conversation with a friend.

The ensuing embarrassment of the blonde, and her insistence on replacing the beer, and the laughter and friendliness of the officer at the situation, was the first meeting of Joyce and John, who some eight years later were destined to become my parents.

Although their initial meeting was so deliciously laced with humour, their relationship was far from a love-match made in heaven. Being the only child of the marriage, and John having died in 1976 and Joyce in 1986, and being myself now in that vague age block of 'over 40', my remembrances of their past and the stories they both told me at different times are somewhat sketchy.

The stories are of course backed up with photographs. One of the most telling perhaps is their November wedding photograph. A wartime wedding in a registry office in 1941, although my mother, with her great sense of flair (both her own parents being dead by this time and she was running her own very successful private hotel), was married from a castle owned by friends in Devon. It's not the clothes in the photograph, though the fact of her wearing all black for her wedding was perhaps indicative of the situation. She looks quite stunning and beautiful, but so sad. My father, immaculate in his lieutenant's uniform, looking tense and so serious. He had totally fallen in love with her at their first meeting, but she at the time was still coming to terms with the great love of her life, Richard, an RAF pilot who had been shot down. She had only agreed to marry my father in the end because he threatened to commit suicide if she didn't.

My own relationship with my mother from around the age of 16 was quite night-marish, and as I now try to tread sensitively and wisely through the minefield of my relationship with my own two daughters, I often ponder over events that happened between her and me, and reflect on how and why she acted in such a manner. And to this end, I think back over her life, particularly up until she met my father. She was 39 when she had me so my own difficult teenage years and her menaupause met head-on in the changing world of the Beatles and the Swinging Sixties. Neither of us stood a chance really, did we? Also now beginning to enjoy the thrills and spills of the menaupause myself, I consider Alison Steadman's portrayal of Mrs. Bennett in the BBC dramatisation of 'Pride and Prejudice'. Presumably if she had been on HRT there would hardly have been a story! Ditto possibly my mother. But no, it is too easy an explanation. I can only see that she had me lined-up to be her chaffeuse/companion, to wait on her hand and foot as she had had to do for the obnoxious and rich old ladies that she had worked for in the early 1930's in Bournemouth. The world was not to be my oyster; but her world was meant to be my cage. It didn't work, needless to say, I fought back and escaped, but not without us both being badly scarred in the process.

I remember reading in an article about mothers and daughters of the over-whelming sense of power that a mother has, as seen from a daughter's eyes. I can remember that feeling towards my mother, and very occasionally I sense a passing presentiment of it with my daughters. As a mother, I have now all the things that they hope to acquire in life, even on the most basic level – a home, a relationship, a certain amount of financial security, but perhaps even more – memories and experiences. On their side, they have youth, energy and beauty and the world truly is their oyster, even if this slightly frightens them. They can do or go anywhere, and be almost anything they want, with the appropriate hard work or whatever it takes.

So how did the once shy and gauche, convent-educated girl from Lincoln come to walk into the pub in Llandudno that night with her puppy and all the charisma of a film-star? I have to say from where I'm standing, it was the start of my life but possibly the closing of the door for many things that she might otherwise have done.

© 2004 Gina Gutteridge

FISH, TURTLES, FLOWERS

It's been a bad morning,
Not even the thirteenth.

The visit to the dentist was grim.
The 'canal root filling' as painful as warned.
The nurse and dentist did not appreciate
Me pushing them away.
'Relax!', he cried severely,
As I lay rigid – almost upside down
With mouth stuffed full of cotton wads.

The final humiliation,
When I howled again
He cried in desperation
'I'm not even doing anything!'.
But it was too late
My body and teeth were
Now on Red Alert
To repel invaders.

We move from
That embarrassing scenario
To the relative peace of a coffee shop,
Where, to my chagrin,
They charged me 45p
For a Mars Bar – marked
Strangely, on my receipt,
As 'buttered toast'!

This, I queried – but it was correct.
Yet, did I have the courage
To say,
'I will not pay such an inflated price
For this unworthy chocolate bar,

Elsewhere available at 29p'.
No, already too bruised with the day.

So, to the final coup de grace
Of this unhappy morning.
On returning to the
Retreat of my car,
Once inside,
What do I spy
But a parking ticket
Plastered over the window.

My unfortunate six twenty pences
Had only registered five
And I had not noticed
On the ticket.
Woe, alas, alack the day.
Should I howl and sob?
And grind my already bruised teeth?

No, because in this morning's post,
A letter –
From faraway, sun-kissed shores,
Telling of hot, hot sun,
Blue sea, blue skies,
Fish, turtles, flowers.

© Gina Gutteridge 25th January, 2002

N.B. *Please note – the Mars bar was not for me!*

GLITTERBUG

I'm all a-glitter!

I have glitter in my hair
Glitter on my skin
Glitter on my nails
Glitter on my lips.

My days are drab
But, come the night
And in my dreams,
I sparkle and shimmer
Like an oriental butterfly.

© Gina Gutteridge 10.10.01

OLD HUNSTANTON BEACH

When I was a little girl, my parents had an elderly friend, a retired prep school headmaster, whose home was full of large watercolour seascapes. These extensive scenes of wind-swept sand-dunes, sea grasses, clouds and the sea in all its moods, were foreign to me, brought up as I was on the south coast with its chalk-white cliffs, pebbly beaches and gentle Downs rolling back from the sea. Foreign to me, that is, until years later, I walked on to Old Hunstanton beach for the first time and looked at that magic sweep of ever-changing sea and sky running towards Thornham and beyond, and the familiar yet unknown vistas of those paintings of years ago, came alive for me.

To the despair of my family, I never tire of that particular beach. Of course, I love the rest of the North Norfolk coast as well, and will happily visit any part at any time. I have been there in all weathers, and at most times of day and night (within reason). From when the lazy Norfolk wind cuts through you mercilessly, to when in high summer, you need a sun-shade or umbrella to prevent sizzling.

I go there when happy and when sad. Alone or in company. We've had family days and picnics there from when the girls were not more than toddlers and they now return at times to walk along the water's edge as confident adults, patting their much shorter mother on the head!

We have strolled and played there with our various dogs through the years. Caley – the beautiful but sadly confused lurcher and Toffee – our present Yorkie-cross and eternal puppy, whose now failing eyesight and hearing have not touched her endless sense of fun and 'hey, let's party' spirit. And long before them, Henry, a beautiful, golden and white retriever-sheepdog cross, with a smile and heart-warming ways that won over all who met him. You ask anyone who knew him - he was a legend in his own time.

When you arrive on the beach by the Coastguard Station, and past The Boathouse Cafe (a life-saver in its own right) for basic 'day on the beach' top-up food, drink and ices (even open on winter weekends for a Sunday roast) there is the major decision. Do you turn right towards Thornham and ever-opening vistas of sea, sand and sky, or do you turn left towards Hunstanton itself? Perhaps make it a circular walk and take in the remains of the wreck in the sand, the flaming orange-pink crumbling cliffs and watch the fulmars, with their stiff-winged soaring flight and their predilection for sitting as if posing for a valentine card, snuggling up oh-so close together. But, annoy them at your peril – for they can be vicious if threatened.

And the sea itself, not just to look at but to get in and on! When the girls were very little, we had a large, rubber dinghy which gave hours of fun. The water quality has varied over the years, but along that particular beach, it has been mainly swimmable. Years when jelly-fish are present add to the interest but the dinner-plate size ones admittably are a bit off-putting.

I think I have swum in the sea almost more this year than any other. One particular day a few weeks ago, when I had visited the beach on my own and, with the low tide, walked quite a way out to get the water level above my knees, and then looked around and realised there was no one else in the water in either direction as far as I could see – nor near the water's edge – I did feel slightly apprehensive and head back for the beach. But otherwise, it is an environment where I feel safe and at home. I was born near the sea and have always lived near the sea, or at least, within driving distance of it, and don't think I could live otherwise. I love it in all its moods. The calm of high summer and the angry foreboding of a rough, winter's day. I also have the greatest respect for the sea and never take any chances with it.

Last August though, was a special day. The hot, sunny weather was truly settled; we had friends staying with us and we all had a wonderful day on the coast, ending up at Old Hunstanton in the late afternoon. We walked to Hunstanton, taking in the unhealthy delights of fresh hot doughnuts, ice-cream and later fish and chips, before making our way slowly back to Old Hunstanton along the sea's edge. The tide was coming in and by the time we were back there it was around 9.30pm, almost high tide, balmy, duskish and quite magical, as only the end of a perfect hot summer's day and evening by the sea can be.

We decided to swim. We had the beach almost to ourselves and in we went. Two in, then myself and a bit of a gap and then my husband. After a while, he called out quietly: "Look behind you".

In the soft dusky light, there was a brown head bobbing about between him and me – but no, not one of our group – a seal! It stayed watching him, then turned to look at me, then did a quick double-take as it realised it was between the two of us and dived. We carried on swimming out a bit further and it bobbed up three more times around us, before finally vanishing. A perfect ending to a perfect day.

However, within less than a month of that unforgettable day, the world was plunged into shock, misery, and gloom with the events of 11th September. A dreadful week and one feared the repercussions. The 18th September was as far removed from the evening of the seal as possible with thrashing rain and wind, cloud and sea mist. I did not want to be at home to see the television a week on from the event and drove to Old Hunstanton to purge some of the thoughts and fears from my system. I felt it was definitely a day of pathetic fallacy and something along the lines of, "All Heaven In A Rage". My thoughts formed themselves into a poem, "Solace". It was a struggle to write in the wind and rain, having searched into the depths of a sodden rucksack and dripping cagoule for pen and paper. A couple walking by nearly bent double peered at the strangely muffled and perching creature sitting on a seat on Hunstanton cliffs trying to write in the downpour, with as many tears pouring down her cheeks as raindrops falling.

But now, another year, time moves on, circumstances change, different joys and sorrows. More often than not now, I go on my own. My family have accepted this need in me for 'my' beach; they are bored stiff with it, and I'm as happy going on my own as with them. I return home relaxed and refreshed, invigorated and inspired – sometimes even with a good tan! What more can you ask?

© 2004 Gina Gutteridge

SOLACE

The sea was solace to my sorrow.
The gulls whirled in the screaming gale and mewed in
    commiseration.
The mist threw a seemly veil over my tears.
Pathetic fallacy was the order of the day.
The day being the 18th September 2001 –
One week on from when the world shook, stood still and
    trembled for its future.

© Gina Gutteridge August, 2002

THE EYES HAVE IT

The mouse with the melting brown eyes
Was equally desired by the black cat, sitting alone, with eyes like
    burning coals,
And the tawny owl, who sat in the oak tree, with eyes like great
    sleepy saucers.
The passing fox with smouldering eyes of chestnut, given the
    chance, would have consumed them all.

But the lurching poacher, with eyes glazed from an evening of
    pub-society,
Saw them all – and passed by without his gun,
Singing his way home, through the misty wood.

© Gina Gutteridge 10.10.01

BLACK MAGIC

Black, black, black – or, as my South African dentist would say, 'blick, blick, blick.' Black-hearted villain. The little black dress. The colour representing death and funerals, yet also strangely, sexual allure. The joke about weddings – the brides wear white (supposedly for purity); the men wear black . . .

I have always loved wearing black and I remember my very first black item of clothing – a black polo-neck jumper. From the pleasure of that first black polo-neck, when I was about fifteen, I don't think I have ever been without one.

I remember a knee-length black cape when I was about nineteen, which I wore and wore, until it fell to pieces. Also, a beautiful black wool military style coat, with a dramatic scarlet lining, which passed down from my much taller mother, made a wonderful maxi-length coat for shorter me. It had epaulets, fixed ties at the wrist, large shiny black buttons and a fur-trimmed collar, which was lovely and snug turned up on a cold day. And, about the same time in my life, a black A-line jersey mini-dress with long fitted sleeves, a mandarin collar, and to make it the so-called 'relieved' black (as opposed to 'unrelieved' black – a strange idea really) a large steel buckle half-belt at the front. But when wearing this dress, did I feel the cat's whiskers, or what!

And talking of cats leads me to black boots. Oh boy, the bliss of my first pair of knee-length, black leather boots, when I was about seventeen – I was walking on air!

Well, if I loved black, I think my mother loved it even more. As a little girl, I was entranced with the unbelievably beautiful, full length, black velvet evening coat, with a cream revere plush velvet collar, that hung in my mother's enormous wardrobe. Occasionally, I would borrow it when I was dressing up and parade around the bedroom feeling like a queen.

The black French, full length evening dress that she wore with it was even more magical. The skirt hung in layers of fine lace and net, with a fitted bodice and sheer net to the neck and full-length sleeves. I also remember an incredibly smart black tailored cocktail dress of fine wool, trimmed with black satin edging.

Then there were the accessories – delightfully small and chic evening bags, full length evening gloves with minute pearl buttons that undid at the wrist, so that you could slip your hand out, rows of smart black court shoes, and, unforgettably, a spray of imitation violets – to go with the furs, as in the song. I remember fresh corsages being used and carefully pinned on, too. No wonder that my father's friends thought he had married a Dior model when he first took her home to Sussex.

What is it that gives black such magic? Well, look at the classic picture of Audrey Hepburn in "Breakfast at Tiffany's", for the ultimate little black dress. Timeless elegance and style lesser mortals can only dream of.

Apart from the inherent mystery somehow exuded by black, it has, too, this amazing slimming quality, which no other colour seems to be able to compete with. It also seems to give a person added authority and perceived stature – somehow saying, "This is me – I am happy with myself – I am in control". Who is actually fooling who is a matter of opinion! Wear black and you immediately feel slimmer, taller, elegant, more authoritative and sexier. What more can you ask of anything?

The allure of wearing black does not only extend to women. A young and very handsome, French-Austrian friend that I had in a previous existence also felt all these things about black – but of course, for his French side, it was the ultimate question of style that mattered so much. Not only did his clothes have to be mainly black (and individually made, because he was around 6ft. 8"), but also I remember a particularly striking gold ring, with a black onyx stone, that he always wore.

Now, I know an ex-pop musician, nudging middle-age, who only ever wears black. Rumour has it that he has been seen in dark grey, but that is now widely believed to be black that has faded!

His devotion to black has continued with a visit to Africa, where he may well have been in grave danger of being seduced by the vibrant and exotic colours found there. But, no, he ordered many items of traditional African clothing in black material, with the added attraction of black embroidery!

So here I am, at forty-plus (I have decided this is my official age for the rest of my life) still devoted to black, with a black polo-neck in the wardrobe, and still getting a big thrill out of buying something truly, madly, deeply black, that just for me, has that extra touch of black magic.

© Gina Gutteridge March, 2003

LINDSAY GUTTERIDGE

Lindsay Gutteridge, in his long and interesting life, has been many things, from a sheep and cattle stationhand in Australia to a graphic designer, lecturer, copywriter, illustrator, photographer, novelist, theatrical set designer and painter. His series of "Dilke" science fiction/spy novels received rave reviews from the Times Literary Supplement, The Telegraph, The Observer and The Sunday Times amongst others, and the Good Book Club said of him: "If he doesn't take Ian Fleming's place he will certainly take the place of John Wyndham". His recreations include travelling, sketching, photography, writing, chess, snooker and amateur dramatics.

BUTTERFLY

She draws back the heavy curtains and grey October light illuminates the room. She stands at the window in her dressing gown, sips her first cup of tea and looks out from her basement flat. Just one room; with a sink and a cooker in an alcove, and the lavatory and bathroom down the passage.

The pavement is at eye-level. Through the area railings she watches the legs and feet of passing office workers, and hears the muted sound of early morning traffic in Brompton Road as it passes the end of the cul-de-sac.

Her letter box rattles, and she shuffles along the passageway and picks up the envelope. The address is in a large sprawling, uneven hand, the stamp is foreign; and she returns to the room with feelings of curiosity and anticipation. She sits by the window and puts on reading glasses. The stamp is Italian, and she opens the envelope with mounting curiosity.

'Ma Cherie,

Here is a voice from the past.

Over the years – so many years – you have been often in my thoughts, and my memories of our singing together are still fresh in my memory: Boheme, Turandot, Traviata, Butterfly... all so long, long ago.

I got your address from an old colleague (Dino Falconi, you will remember him) when I met him by chance during an interval at La Scala – where I go sometimes (it's the God's for me now!) as I live in the country only a bus ride from Milan...'

As she reads, she sees him clearly, the big, handsome Paul Pasolini; and she wipes her misted reading glasses with a forefinger – then she goes to her escritoire, takes up a pen and writes:

'My Dearest Paul,

Oh! how happy your letter has made me! What a lovely surprise!!

How the memories come flooding back!!!

My Dear, I'm afraid that we old singers have only our memories to live on now. I wonder what our lives would

have been like if we had stayed together? – but a marriage would never have lasted. Why were we always fighting? I have never married – have you? Have you children, are you well, are you happy ???
It's so lovely to hear from you!
If ever you are in London...
With love from Mimi, Violetta, Gilda – and Dorothia.'
He wrote again.
She wrote again.
He wrote:
'Darling, I am flying to London tomorrow, leaving Milan in the morning; and plane, tube and bus should bring me to you mid-afternoon.
In haste, much love — Paulo.'

She spends the day in nervous anticipation; buys food and flowers, hoovers and dusts and plumps-up cushions; and at the sound of the doorbell she glances quickly into the mirror and hurries along the passage.

They have changed more than they had anticipated, and for a moment they are silent; then thy embrace with exclamations of pleasure.

He is still a man of the theatre, and wears a big, black Fedora and a long black coat slung around his shoulders – but his black hair is now white, his shoulders stooped, and the hand which presents a bouquet trembles just a little.

She adds his roses to her vase of flowers; takes his hat and coat and sits him down. And she fusses... there is tea or coffee – or something stronger? "How lovely to see you! Did you have a good trip? How I envy you Italy... Oh! the weather in London. How lovely to see you."

Gradually, over coffees, they become more relaxed. And, inevitably, they talk of old times; of Rome and Glynebourne and The Met. The walls of the room are hung with yellowing posters and faded photographs.

Their names are in bold type beneath the names of operas in which they were the principal performers. Photographs show them with conductors of legendary reputation. They rise from the sofa and walk and talk from picture to picture. Do you remember? Do you remember? Do you remember...

They pause before a Japanese fan pinned to the wall, and they sing. They sing together, their voices thin and tremulous. He with an arm around her waist, the other arm flung wide; she with clasped hands, head laid back and eyes closed.

She is Butterfly and he is Pinkerton: they sing to the sound of tumultuous applause from a vast auditorium; then there is silence. They turn and look sadly into each other's eyes.

"My darling", she says, "I have more than pictures from the past. I have something special for you which I've treasured for more than half a century" and she goes to a cupboard and slides back a door to reveal a gramophone and a small pile of records, from which she takes a record, draws it from its paper dust-cover and holds it up between her fingertips.

"It is you. And it is me" she smiles "...and it is 'Butterfly'".

As she turns to put the disk on the turntable, he leans towards her and says quietly, "May I see?".

He takes the record to examine the faded, gold lettering on the orange label, "An old 78", he murmurs.

"Deutsche Grammophon", he reads.

"'Madam Butterfly' by Giacomo Puccini... in Italian... The Vienna Philharmonic Orchestra conducted by Herbert Von Karajon."

His voice becomes a whisper, "Dorothia Jansson: Soprano. Paulo Pasolini: Tenor."

She reaches out silently and he passes the record to her.

Their hands tremble. The record slips through her fingers and falls.

The brittle record splinters into a thousand fragments.

© 2004 Lindsay Gutteridge

OLSON

Carl Olson settled in England after losing his job as wireless operator with a Swedish shipping company. A tiff with the first mate led to fisticuffs, summary dismissal and being dumped ashore at Liverpool.

Over the years, Olson became a recluse with a hobby. He collected old wireless sets; returning from auction sales with Bushes, Pyes, Murphies, Fergusons and G.E.C's until his house in Bethlehem Terrace was full of them – all switched on from breakfast to suppertime; mostly playing dozens of different stations, sometimes blasting out Wagner or Beethoven in unison.

For years his neighbours complained bitterly to the rent collector, but all the satisfaction they got was 'Sorry, none of my business' and 'Sort it out for yourselves'

So when the Johnsons and the O'Hearns, Olson's next-door neighbours, heard the news that Bethlehem Terrace was to be demolished and its tenants rehoused in a new block of flats, they had reason to celebrate – there'd be no more of that bloody racket pounding through the bloody party walls!

There had been a dozen houses in Bethlehem Terrace and there were twelve floors in Bethlehem Towers; the title given by Liverpool's Housing Superintendent, a compassionate man, who thought that retaining the name 'Bethlehem' might reduce the trauma the tenants would feel on losing their cosy old homes – in fact the tenants of Bethlehem Terrace clapped their hands at the prospect of having new kitchens and bathrooms and a view right across Liverpool to the Irish coast. The Superintendent saw the Towers as a vertical reincarnation of the old horizontal terrace, in which all the old good-neighbourliness would continue as before when old friends who had lived side by side were housed above and below each other in the new building. So the Johnsons and O'Hearns still had Carl Olson as a neighbour; and as Bethlehem Towers was a low-budget building with minimal sound-proofing between floors the noise was worse than ever.

The response by the housing authority to their angry complaints was to urge them to live and let live, and try to show compassion for a lonely, friendless old man; but most of Tower's residents had little sympathy for him. The children, taking their cue from their parents, chased after him and mimicked his accent and scrawled swear-words on his front door; to which Olson responded with rude gestures and Swedish obscenities – and went on buying and playing old wireless sets.

Returning from the pub one Saturday afternoon, Johnson and O'Hearn found Olson, with his latest purchase, climbing the stairs ahead of them.

There was an angry confrontation, and words led to actions. O'Hearn grabbed the radio and the tug-of-war finished with Irishman and radio tumbling to the bottom of the stairs, with the radio smashed and O'Hearn concussed.

Olson hurried to his flat and slammed the door and Johnson called an ambulance.

A month later Olson was charged with assault. In court, his neighbours gave a rather slanted account of their encounter, accusing him of knocking O'Hearn down the stairs without provocation, and his anti-social history influenced the magistrates to take a serious view of his behaviour. He was sent to prison, and spent six months in custody, morosely listening through ear-plugs to music from his Walkman radio.

During his spell in jail, his flat was let to new tenants and his radios were consigned to a council skip.

He found lodgings and spent his days wandering the streets, sitting in public parks, eating in cheap cafes... always with eyes downcast, in a world apart, listening to his Walkman. A double-decker hit him as he was crossing the road (to the sound of violins) to the Albert Memorial.

The ambulance man felt no pulse at wrist or neck — but was there a whisper from his heart, a faint irregular beat? The ambulance man put an ear to Carl Olson's chest. It was not his heart: it was his Walkman. And it was not a requiem: it was The Sex Pistols.

© 2004 Lindsay Gutteridge

SYMPHONY FOR CUPBOARD DOORS – AND A LIGHT BULB

Yesterday I hunted for old letters and photographs in drawers and cupboards in my bedroom/T.V. room.

This morning I awake and sit up in bed as the sun comes peeping in at dawn.

My dressing gown jumps off the hook on the back of my bedroom door and heads for the bathroom, and the door closes behind him.

The doors on the built-in wardrobe are open. Two sets of doors, big ones at the bottom and small ones for the cupboards above.

A little door swings-to and shuts with a click and so does its twin, then they open simultaneously to the sound of music as my little bedside radio switches on. The big doors follow suit and all of them start a jolly gavotte as the curtains at the window swish together – and the hanging light bulb glows into life.

"No! No!" I protest "Please let the sun in", and the curtains open again. But the light stays on, increases to 150 watt brilliance, and swings to the rhythm of the cupboard dance. Inside the wardrobe my multi-coloured shirts jig about on their hangers and ties slither off their tie-rack and snake about on the writhing carpet patterns. My pillow moves and sighs and the duvet moves in gentle waves.

Up in the wardrobe cupboard a shoe-box opens and a package of letters from family, old friends and sweethearts slides out and the pink ribbon bow on the package comes undone. Yellowing pages of faded writing ascend to the ceiling, and a shelf-full of Penguin paperbacks take wing and flap around the light bulb which goes up and down to the rhythm of a Radio Two waltz.

The television screen at the foot of the bed glows into life. There are voices: it's a T.V. chat show, and the host and hostess look out, see the flying Penguins and get out to have a better view. They're only little people, a few inches tall, sitting together on top of the set.

A moth and a wasp flapping and buzzing against the windowpane are joined by the paperbacks; the sash window slides slowly down and off they swoop into the sunshine; the old letters descend from the ceiling and float after them. The ties on the carpet get under the bed.

The curtains draw together. All is darkness. A dirge on Radio Three follows Radio Two. The show is ended. The dressing gown opens the door and sits on the edge of the bed. "Why are you in the dark?" he says.

He switches off the radio. "I hate Mahler. Can't stand him!" he says.

© 2004 Lindsay Gutteridge

PAMELA PALMER

Pamela Palmer lives in and loves West Norfolk. As a long term member of the King's Lynn Writers' Circle she has written – in addition to short stories – several crime novels, children's stories, scripts and plays. One of her plays, "Heavenly Bodies," was performed in Cambridge by the Menagerie Theatre. She has also written articles for craft magazines and reviews for the local press.

DAUGHTER OF THE FOREST

A small wild bird flew up into the sky screaming and reeling. Under it a melody drifted upwards. It came from a girl seated on a tree stump between the edge of a field and a woodland of beech trees. This woodland was the farthest corner of a vast forest that spread behind her covering the rolling countryside.

A man stepped out of the beech woods, his gun hoisted against his shoulder. It was pointed at the bird in the sky. The girl didn't scream vacantly, instead she rose from her seat and ran rhythmically towards the man. She slung her slender body at him. The gun fired without a target and the two people tumbled into the ferns.

Panic seemed to have transferred itself from the bird to her. She turned to the wood and started to run.

The hunter followed her, his quarry. She turned briefly, panting. She wove between the trees – a gazelle of the forest. She seemed to know her way by instinct. Brambles plucked at her hair and clothes.

The ground threaded more slowly beneath the gazelle's feet. Her keen ears could hear his breathing. She halted, leaned against a tree and saw the intent in her victor's eyes, and smiled. She knew him and she wanted him.

At first the gazelle and the hunter crouched like wild things, but the summer sunshine calmed them and warmed their now naked skin. A cradle of last year's leaves formed around her body and she forgave the world. The hunter took his prey.

As the sky darkened the hunter left the woodland his gun slung under his arm. The skylarks were asleep in the meadow grass and the girl was on her way home to her father's tied cottage.

The girl knew what would greet her there. It was a place where people weren't supposed to dream. The hours twirled the hands of the clock and the function of the household rotated with likewise regularity. She knew the kitchen would be filled by four figures at the table. They would be moving their knives and forks in a silent reverence performed over the meal before them.

She thought of the bookcase in the corner of the front room, the only acknowledgement of another way of living. But there were no works of imagination or entertainment among its dry contents except, perhaps, for the Bible.

The rain started to come down in fat blobs. She waited until one of the figures from the kitchen came outside and turned into a strong youth chopping wood in his shirtsleeves.

'Arganna,' said the youth smiling. As he turned it became obvious that manhood was upon him. 'Have you been misbehaving again?'

His sister smiled as she settled herself on a log in the woodshed. Arganna blew a raindrop from her nose and said, 'Garth,' in a gentle, reproving voice. She examined his face as he toiled with an axe. The warmth of his body protected it from the rain. His physical activity gave him the look of an archangel full of honest energy. It seemed to Arganna that his life's confusions were reduced to an axe and a piece of wood. He stopped and shook his head.

'You aren't simple, yet you behave as if the horrors of the world will never touch you. We live in this world, Arganna. You cannot become part of the forest or meadow.'

'I have always been that, Garth, but now I am part of something else. A kind of passion for the life around me. I'm part of that.'

Garth frowned. Arganna laughed, ran down the garden and went back into the forest.

Now she knew her body to be that of a woman's and the trees' scent was as strong as her own. Her clothes stuck to her, wet from the rain, but warm from her body. She ran through the wood to the hunter's cottage.

By the time she got there the rain had stopped and steam was rising from the undergrowth. She peeled off her clothes and hung them on the bushes to dry. With the freedom of her nakedness she approached the moon. Her faith in her body sent her into the clearing. She went to the door but no-one answered. The windows were blank. The vacancy of the cottage started to fill her with emptiness. She backed off. The forest covered her.

Reflections of shadows ponded the forest. Having surrendered her shoes, she watched her feet feel the texture of the summer mud. She leant towards the moon and prayed a thanksgiving for her womanhood. She ran her hand over her body and felt it for the first time. It pleased her as it had pleased the hunter.

The muddy path took her to the edge of the forest where the moon was unhindered by the branches of the trees. Bats crisscrossed the sky and a little owl screeched into the night. Her mother would fear this – the night. Her father would fight it. She wanted to be a part of it.

Two people were walking along the edge of the forest. Arganna leaned against a tree – not to hide, but to watch. They fumbled with each other's clothes unperturbed by their lack of expertise, and tumbled to the ground. But the trappings of the outside world encumbered their passion until the girl remembered her other existence and her passion died.

Arganna saw them go. Suddenly her body chilled. She returned to her clothes and covered herself. They felt stiff and tight, but they had the perfume of the forest. She lay under the trees and slept with the depth and ferocity that satisfied her exhaustion.

High summer had gone and the trees were sleeping. In the forester's cottage voices were raised. Arganna crept out of the house. The forest beckoned. Frost had formed on the branches and icy spirals caught the moonlight. The silence was unbroken.

She ran her fingers over her rounded shape and breathed the cold air for two hearts now instead of just her own.

'We are suffocating in that house. We cannot live there,' she told the forest. It didn't answer. The leaves beneath her feet were hard, but she lay on them and looked up into the silvered branches. 'Take us,' she said and closed her eyes.

Emotional pain enticed her away from reality into a yawning vastness of possibilities. Even the possibility of complete nothingness caressed her mind. 'Let go. Leave life behind. Follow those that have gone before. Leave life to the fighters, the winners. Losing is easy – it's just a warm caressing void,' her misery seemed to say.

A light swam by. Perhaps it was a warning, or a beacon to an escaping soul. But obligatory form crept into the shadows, feeling it's way through the glorious chaos of her decision against life. Before her, three fingers grasped a lantern – its square window divided the light equally through four panes of glass. It gave the light she'd seen.

She could see other lights: the outlined shapes of moon and stars making ancient patterns, living patterns, not the beguiling patterns of death. A small point of light was now inside her begetting more light, forming flowers of beauty she would not take from the world.

She would not be as one with nature, not this time. The rhythm of the inner life growing inside her was asserting itself, giving her strength and a new unity, no patterns of destruction could touch this creation.

Arganna clenched the frosted leaves with bare hands. Her dress was frozen and her legs and feet naked. She let her family take her from that place to a bedroom where the fireplace lay vacant and the sheets were neither aired nor warm.

The shivering started as she gave herself up to the living. The silent figure of her mother touched the bed. As she slept her hands opened and the forest leaves, now warm and damp, fell to the floor. On waking, Arganna could hear her family whispering downstairs. She felt cleansed. Her pregnancy remained. It was part of her. She smiled.

The spring sunshine poured through the coloured windows. Arganna caressed her now large mound as she stood among the Sunday congregation, the only member of her family there. The others had come to an earlier service. An uneasy gentleness coated the pews. The sun's borrowed colours only partly mellowed the fears of the churchgoers.

Arganna stared at the religious artefacts: ancient, explanatory, lonely pieces of wood. She touched a carved pew. Was it love or craftsmanship, faith or employment that had created its beauty?

The cathedralled timbers soared skywards. They were imposing, but they did not move her soul as the forest did. Her maker was in the forest. Her love was in the forest. Her hunter had been in the forest.

She walked homewards. The air was different by the forest, astringent and still. Arganna breathed it in and spoke to the trees.

'Your balance fulfilled my emotions. But you have taken me and made me a forest creature. My family think me crude because I do what my body wants. They fight what their bodies want. Yet I have nothing now other than this baby.' She wept with anger. Had she been so willingly cheated, she wondered. She pounded her fists into the trunk of a beech tree, and ran into the wood, her feet trying to punish the ground.

At the edge of the woodland the brambles had started to grow across the path and the burden inside her moved endlessly. It sat against her ribs and restricted her breathing. Torn and tired she slid down by a brown-green trunk, closed her eyes and listened to the squirrels moving in the branches.

Somewhere inside her a part of her body moved which had never moved in that way before. Arganna smiled. The forest was working its magic. She started to remove her clothes to feel the forest air against her body. Inside her the movement came again. It was not strong enough to take the smile from her. She crouched down and rubbed a handful of new leaves across her distended abdomen.

While above her the leaves at the top of each tree turned back and forth changing shades of spring-green with every turn. Below, Arganna crawled through the leaf mould until, still able to smile, she reached the tree where she had watched the woodland lovers by night.

The movement inside lurched at her, this time throwing her off balance and taking her breath away. She held onto her tree. The pain had taken over her former ecstasy. Her mouth opened to grasp the air. She filled her lungs and yelled, 'Mother,' into the forest. It was a tormented rejection of her fate.

As the sound faded a small grey figure moved through the trees towards her silently carrying a bundle of blankets. 'I heard you,' said Arganna's mother.

'I wasn't calling you,' said Arganna as the wave of pain left her.

'I know,' said her mother.

'You are so tight, mother. Part of you wants to be like me. The other part wants to be what everyone else wants you to be, and that is the part you have given yourself up to. Yet the forest is natural, naked, clean, bold. I want to be like the forest. I want the baby to be the same. I don't want to be tangled in every day life so we can't move and think.'

'My forest child,' said her mother, smiling. She waited while her daughter writhed from another contraction and stroked the girl's tangled hair. 'It is always like this. Tomorrow it will all be over and you will have brought a new life into the world. Work hard and it will soon be over.'

Arganna pulled a living branch growing on a young tree towards her. She bit it hard, her teeth grinding into it with each contraction. She delivered her baby into the forest.

The baby girl suckled at her breast while the baby's grandmother wrapped blankets around them. As the baby fed Arganna felt warm and her heart was quiet, so quiet it would not disturb the baby that suckled so close to it.

'Motherhood is potent and peaceful like the forest,' said Arganna.

'My sweet girl, before, you were like a wren in the winter hedgerow, looking for grubs that were not there. But you brightened our hearts. You are a child of nature. Motherhood will suit you. Every other burden is light compared to raising a new life. You will need your forest many times to give you strength.'

'I feel the power of the forest, the strength of creation. Everything comes from that,' said Arganna.

The forest barely stirred in comment. Half curled ferns pushed up at the edge of the forest like loyal centuries awaiting their summer duties. The fallen branches littering the ground from last winter's gales rotted silently. While, below, unseen roots gave rise to the ancient timber around the women, keeping quiet secrets it had known for a hundred years. Only a whisper came from the leaves being cherished by the afternoon sun.

The End

© 2004 Pamela Palmer

HALFWAY HOUSE

'Inspector Forester, I'm Mrs Parson. I run this place for my employers. You may have heard of the company?' She handed me a card, but I didn't recognise the name. I slipped the card into my jacket pocket.

I had already seen Alice's body in her bedroom with the forensic team working around her, now myself and my colleague, DC Barron, were being shown from the stairs into the dining room by the housekeeper of this halfway house.

'We've never had anything like this happen before,' said the piping voice of our hostess. Mrs Parson's perfectly made up face and compact body moved easily to the dining room door as if her forty plus years were no burden to her. I imagined this woman smoothly moving into a different gear to fit every circumstance. A dead body with a carving knife struck through its heart appeared to be only another household duty to deal with. But, perhaps, that was what it was like in these places.

'Mary,' explained Mrs Parson, showing me into the dining room. Mary was a large inmate slumped across the table. Her curly tousled hair lay across her forearm, until she looked up.

She looked as shaken as all the inmates I'd ever seen in these places. With a wan, hopeful smile she shook hands. She must've seen me as a powerful person with my height and my dark hair scraped back to make my features look sharp. How wrong she was.

I could see Mary needed more than more than anyone could ever give her. The shutters went up behind my eyes. No more pain was going to be dragged out of me.

'Alice was my friend, Inspector,' said Mary. 'I loved her. She had the face of an angel.'

'It's all right, Mary. I know … but I have to talk to you about all this. It's my job. You don't have to call me "Inspector", call me, "Jenny". I've asked Mrs Parson to stay; though she may not help you with your answers. DC Barron is here to take notes.' I sounded reassuring. Mary snivelled loudly. She wiped her hand across her nose and Mrs Parson passed the girl a tissue.

'I'm sorry,' said Mrs Parson to me.

'She has a right to grief,' I replied, and I wondered what Mary's psychiatric record contained.

She started to talk through her blubbing. 'My room's next to Alice's.' She sniffed. 'I was chatting with her in her room until late. The clock said eleven-thirty. We were both tired so I went to my own bed.'

'Good,' said Mrs Parson to Mary.

I frowned and said, 'Mrs Parson, please keep quiet.' Then I turned to Mary. 'Had you quarrelled with Alice?' I asked.

''Course I hadn't,' Mary replied. Her gaze started to flick around the room, but she could not run away. There was no exit. DC Barron used his large body and sturdy legs to shadow the dining room door while Mrs Parson sat by the window.

'I found her,' said Mrs Parson, 'trying to get out in the middle of the night, rattling doors and windows but everything was locked up.'

'Please don't interfere with my questioning, Mrs Parson,' I said to her, and then I turned to Mary. 'Did you do as Mrs Parson says? Did you go around rattling windows?'

'I had a bad dream,' she replied. 'I dreamt Alice was stabbed and the murderer was chasing me.'

'Do you remember what this murderer looked like?' I asked.

'It was a dark shape with a dagger. It was a dream.' Mary's eyes seemed to sink back into her skull.

'That's fine, Mary, dear. You go and make us a cup of tea. We'll sort this out. Don't you worry.' Mrs Parson's voice soothed the girl, who smiled weakly back at her.

'Mrs Parson, that is quite enough,' I said.

Mrs Parson assessed me. I hid behind my slightly less than fashionable clothes so my body was not under scrutiny in addition to my personality. Remaining seated prevented my height from intimidating her. I twiddled my counterfeit wedding ring and stared back at her. Did she see through to my insecure centre?

The halfway house manager finished looking and turned away saying, 'Mary has been violent. She's schizophrenic, but I make sure she takes her medication regularly. She's not had a relapse as long as she's been here.'

I looked down, away from the present and back to the past. I could hear my mother's voice in my head. "The pills are killing me." She'd said it over and over again. But she'd needed those pills.

'Do you want to see the next one, dear?' asked Mrs Parson. Her voice tried to gather me into her fold. It was ridiculous. We were the same age. She could not mother me as she so obviously did her residents. I was prepared to tolerate it though. If I allowed her to be herself she would possibly reveal more.

'There were only five residents in, dear,' continued Mrs Parson. 'Six were out for the weekend and none of those had keys. Out of the ones that were left two take sleeping pills regularly. These are administered by myself, so they wouldn't have been able to do anything but sleep. You've seen Mary. That leaves Gloria and Denis.'

'And yourself,' I added. Mrs Parson smiled at what she assumed to be my little joke.

When Denis came in to the dining room he was grinning at a joke he'd made privately to himself. It made his large black glasses jiggle on his thin nose. He looked at me sideways on. I knew he would not be telling me his joke. I guessed his age at twenty-five.

'I read detective stories,' he said, and pushed his glasses back into position with his middle finger. He took out a cigarette with twitching fingers.

Always the twitching fingers, I remembered my mother's twitching fingers. I glanced away.

He asked, 'Do you mind if I smoke?'

I thought he'd misunderstood my revulsion. It wasn't the smoking I objected to. I shook my head. 'Please, carry on,' I said.

Denis lit his cigarette. 'I went to the moon last night,' said Denis. 'I fought a gale of wind in my room with a sword. It disappeared down the sink dragging me in its vortex all the way.' He waved his cigarette above his head as if pointing to a moon that was not now there.

'That's enough Denis,' said Mrs Parson. He pulled his knees up, placing his feet on the edge of the dining room chair. He rested his chin on his knees. 'The truth, Denis.'

I let her tackle his wayward mind, but I tried to follow his words for hidden meanings.

'The truth? What is the truth?' he answered the home manager. 'Is it reality? A dream can seem like reality, but is a dream a truth?'

'Denis,' scolded Mrs Parson.

'What was Alice like, Denis?' I asked.

'She accepted the truth of her animal instincts. Her sexual appetite was corrupting. Her brilliance was unrepentant. Her beauty was organic and her life was vibrant, but she was an instrument of evil. I made love to her five times a day.' Denis unravelled his legs and addressed Mrs Parson, 'Lying on the bed, all forgiveness, have you forgotten the blissful ease of lies?'

'That's enough, Denis,' snapped Mrs Parson.

'We die easily. Give us a noose or a railway line, a busy road. They know how to get rid of us.'

I knew what he meant. Suicide was never far away. My mother had died by her own hand, her pills untaken in the bathroom cabinet.

'I was listening to the radio and fell asleep. I heard nothing until morning,' said Denis. His voice was flat with finality. I told him he could go so he rose and left, leaving his cigarette stubbed out on the table.

Mrs Parson went to fetch Gloria only to find she'd been sedated by the doctor who was just leaving by the front door. I heard the conversation as I manoeuvred my way into the kitchen for a drink.

Mary wasn't there but the pot of tea she'd made was, so I poured out two cups. DC Barron had followed without question and was standing by the back door. His body still stiff and straight, he showed me the contents of a file he'd brought with him – the social services' records. Then he took his cup of tea.

I glanced round, the place was immaculate. I opened the dishwasher. It was a credit to Mrs Parson's efficiency. The kitchen door opened behind me.

'I meant to warn you that Denis is unreliable. He makes things up all the time. His imagination is quite out of control,' said Mrs Parson.

'It has always struck me how cruelly accurate the nearly insane tend to be, Mrs Parson,' I replied.

'The boy talks in riddles. Unfortunately, people cannot sympathise with a disease of the mind like they can for a disease of the body. But he is really only an over-grown naughty child.' Mrs Parson smiled and hugged her arms across her bosom.

Tapping the file, I said, 'Mrs Parson, you said that this sort of thing has never happened before, but there have been several sudden deaths here while you've been in charge.'

'Yes dear, there has. One walked onto the railway line, another walked out in front of a car, and old Gerald plugged himself into the mains. They were all suicides. No one has been stabbed before.'

'What was Alice like?' I asked, changing tack.

'She was a different person to everyone. She was whatever they wanted her to be. Mary wanted a friend, Denis wanted a temptress, Gloria wanted a mother figure, though they were nearly the same age.' Mrs Parson studied her peach coloured nails.

'And what was she for you?' I searched her tepid blue eyes. They avoided me.

'I'm only the house manager here. I just see to the business of the house, keep it running. She didn't interfere with that.'

What right had Mrs Parson to talk to me as if I were a meddlesome daughter? My mother had gone. I turned and looked out of the kitchen window only to see an image of myself wrestling with my mother, my hand cut by the razor blade she held. I had wanted her to die to save me the pain of her life, but I couldn't have let her kill herself. But on another day she had tricked me, and had succeeded in taking her own life.

I looked back into the room to lose the memory and got up to go. Someone else could finish this investigation, I couldn't cope with my past being stirred up inside me. Then the confusion of voices

I'd heard – Mary, Denis, Mrs Parson and my mother – settled in my mind. I knew their complicated thought pattern, the destructive contortions of their logic. I turned on Mrs Parson.

'I have a job to do and you are not helping in any way whatsoever. This can only indicate to me your guilt in this matter. Surely other halfway houses do not have the death rate yours has?' I tapped the folder. 'The residents were feeling drowsy and falling asleep last night, Mary and Denis said so. You must have drugged Alice, Mary and Denis last night as well as those that usually have sleeping draughts and, perhaps, Gloria too. I have arranged blood tests that will show any traces of sleeping drugs left in them.'

Mrs Parson sat down. She put her over made-up face into her square hands. 'I gave them all sleeping draughts last night. I needed the rest. I have help, but the job is hard. I'd changed the brand of sleeping draught and Mary reacted badly to it and had that dreadful nightmare.' She looked at her hands again. 'I fear Alice may have done the same and killed her self,' she added.

We were interrupted by a knock on the door, followed by a large woman in white overalls letting herself in. She passed me a piece of paper with her large writing sprawled all over it. 'I thought you'd want to know,' she said.

I thanked the head of the forensic team. This information couldn't have come at a better time.

'The forensic people have examined Alice's room,' I said. 'You washed up all the mugs – I saw them in the dishwasher – but one of the residents didn't drink his or her milk drink. Cocoa residues were found in Alice's sink. Was it Alice's cocoa, or someone else's? Did Alice sleep a drugged sleep?' I paused letting the facts and their implications settle on Mrs Parson. Then I added, 'You must have heard what went on last night, Mrs Parson?'

'I love them. I want to look after them. I can do that, protect them from the world. My sweet little Gloria needed a mother.' Her tongue savoured the name. 'She didn't need Alice. She needed me.'

'You didn't love Alice?' I asked.

'She wouldn't be mine. And she enticed them away from me,

especially my girl. Don't you see?' Mrs Parson looked at me with watering eyes and said, 'I had to kill her.'

'You didn't kill Alice, Mrs Parson. It was the person who failed to drink the cocoa. You know who it is, don't you? You have corrupted the evidence in each of these cases of sudden death.' I stopped. A small blond girl stepped into the kitchen.

'Gloria,' gasped Mrs Parson. 'Go back to bed.'

'I was at each of those deaths, but Mrs Parson always said I was with her,' said Gloria. 'I was at the railway line and the road and with the old man. I showed them how to find what they really wanted.' The girl produced a large round tablet and laid it on the table. 'I don't need sedatives — or any pills. I can avoid taking tablets any time I want to.' She turned to accuse Mrs Parson, 'You never notice.'

'What happened last night, Gloria?' I asked.

'When I heard Mary leave Alice's room I went in. I knew the cocoa was drugged and Alice would soon be asleep. I poured my cup down the sink. The voices told me to do it.'

'What voices?' I asked, but I knew. The same inner voices that had made my mother destroy herself. 'What did they make you do?'

'They said if I did as they told me they would take me away to a peaceful place,' said Gloria. 'They told me who to kill and I killed Alice.' She smiled, pleased with herself. Her face changed to loathing when she looked at Mrs Parson. 'It's easy to get round her.'

Mrs Parson wept bitterly digging her fingers into her scalp.

'Denis mentioned your lies, Mrs Parson,' I said. 'He even said that Mary's dream was what really happened, in his own way – being chased and being told what to do. Who was telling Gloria to do what she did? Her voices were feeding off what she'd been told. These people needed your help. But you had power over them and you enjoyed making them yield to that, didn't you?'

'I wanted my residents to be mine, Inspector. It was easy to let Gloria kill them if any of them tried to undermine my authority. I could tell her which ones I didn't like. Her poor mind would work on that information. By covering for her I kept her mine.'

DC Barron called in other officers who, with him, cautioned Mrs Parson and took her into custody. Gloria was taken into the dining room while a social worker and a doctor could be found.

When we started to leave Mrs Parson pulled at my sleeve and asked, 'How did you know?'

'Mothers manipulating their children is not new,' I said and I tugged my jacket from her.

Denis was leaning against the front door. 'A palpating brain, a deafened heart, while pain enlarges the soul – weary, groaning, mourning. Grief hasten through you and leave you clean. Let it take its bitterness from you and leave you alone.' His voice was dreamy. I felt penetrated. He saw me and knew my past, my lost battle with my mother's insanity.

'It's the guilt, Denis. I wanted to save my mother and couldn't. The grief has long gone.'

He moved away from the door and touched my hand. I slid through into the sunlight. The door closed behind me shutting my past away with it. This place had been my halfway house. Its misery had stirred my own miseries and forced me to look at them. They would never frighten me again.

© 2004 Pamela Palmer

PATRICIA WALTON

Patricia Walton was born and grew up in Newcastle upon Tyne. She is a writer of women's contemporary fiction. Her three published paperbacks, 'To Forget The Past', 'A Woman Like Me' and 'A Friend Like Me', are set in Northumbria.

Patricia's next novel is set in Norfolk where, for the past thirty years, she has lived with her husband, Alan, dividing her time between writing and family life.

THE WOMAN ON THE BEACH

Kate came to live in the white bungalow in November, a time of year when strangers were a rarity, arousing curiosity, resentment by some who, unreservedly, classified anyone living near the beach in the worst of the winter months, an oddity.

As she neither knew them nor desired their approval, if the truth were known, the local cognoscenti were the least of her problems. It was food or, more precisely, lack of it that drove her to the village shops when, mercifully, the bone chilling easterlies scaled down their aggression to bearable, the sun shone and common sense prevailed. She could withstand a winter in her grandfather's old beach bungalow, cope with being alone in a wilderness of space, defying wild coastal elements, but not without food.

Comforting herself with thoughts of a proper meal along with sorely needed exercise a walk to the shops entailed, she picked up a warm coat and two shopping bags.

Outside the newsagent's shop, Kate paused, braced herself for Mr Hedley's wide-eyed surprise on seeing her. Bushy eyebrows raised a notch or two, his nervous little cough and tentative smile usually the prelude to variations on 'You still living along the beach, Miss?'

As if the whole village didn't know where she lived. What's more, she objected to his assumption that she was a spinster! No doubt trying to be friendly, but Mr Hedley's interest in her affairs, whether kindly meant or not, only served to stiffen her resolve to tough it out at the bungalow. She'd know when the time was right for her to leave.

Clutching bars of dark chocolate, a Norfolk Journal and today's Guardian, she thanked the newsagent and paid him before heading for the butcher, the baker, the ... a smile curled her lips. Becoming acclimatized to a life without electricity but a vain hope.

Coming out of the hardware store into a dank, drizzly mist she thought poor exchange for the earlier fresh, salty air, Kate turned her coat collar higher round her neck, pulled a black woollen hat over her ears and with a laden shopping bag in each hand, retraced her steps. Passing the school playing field and The Vicarage, she was nearing the Crown & Anchor when she spotted "the watcher on the beach."

'They look heavy,' he called, walking towards her. 'Here, let me carry them back for you,' he offered, taking the bags from her hands before she'd time to object.

'What is it you find so interesting on the beach? Can't be me.'

He laughed, completely unperturbed by her abrupt manner. 'No, not you. Sure, I see you out and about now and then, but around this time it's migratory birds that drag me out of my bed on frosty mornings. I notice you're an early riser.'

Taller, younger looking this close and surprisingly, quietly spoken. From London, Kate guessed, curbing a smile. Like me, 'he 'int local,' they would say hereabouts.

'With no elecricity, what d'you do for heat and light down there?'

Slightly bemused by his interest in her comfort, she said, 'Bottled gas, an oil lamp and candles,' immediately swinging the conversation away from her and back to his all-consuming interest. 'On one of my early morning walks, I saw the geese, so many they filled the sky.'

It was their noisy chatter that made her stop, look up and there she'd stayed rooted to the spot til they passed and the sky became blue again. Such a breathtaking sight she could almost believe observing birds a valid reason for him spending so much time near her bungalow.

'There'd be too many to count, that's for sure. There's nothing like the sky filled with skein after skein of chattering pink-footed geese flying out over the marshes after an overnight roost.'

Garden birds she knew something about, but this, ornithologically speaking, was a different world of which he seemed very knowledgeable, so genuinely hooked on the subject, she could be wrong about him, so stayed silent, could hardly show her ignorance by admitting that, at first glance, she thought they were swans.

They reached the sprawl of empty holiday homes and stopping,

Kate thanked him. "I'll manage fine from here.'

'My pleasure. It's a long, dark road to walk on your own in winter, Mrs Ferguson.'

Mrs Ferguson? Tight-lipped, Kate stared at him, her carefully measured words masking her resentment. 'You have me at a disadvantage. Yes, I'm Kate Ferguson. Who are you?'

'Sergeant Mike Tasker.' He smiled. 'A policeman, and knowing who's living here at this time of year makes my job easier. I see you've no landline and without electricity couldn't recharge your mobile, so the odd occasion could arise when you need a helping hand.'

'I was right. It is more than pink-footed geese you keep an eye on and I wonder why. If you've been listening to the local bush telegraph, I'm probably either a criminal on the run or an asylum escapee when I'm nothing more interesting than a woman struggling to fight her way back to a semblance of her normal self.'

'I don't listen to gossip, but I do have a duty to the vulnerable and living alone on the beach, you are at the mercy of the tides.'

The policeman had his job to do, she conceded, marginally less annoyed. After all, he knew nothing about her or why she had to live here, but if he'd put two and two together might've guessed a woman who leaves her home, her friends, all she'd ever known and loved to live in this wintry outpost, she could, possibly, take care of herself.

'Goodbye, Mrs Ferguson. Take care.'

'I appreciate your kindness,' she replied automatically, wondering if she sounded as anti-everything as she felt. Dumping her bags on the floor of the living room, Kate collapsed into the only comfortable chair in the bungalow and thought of her grandpa. He lived in Norwich most of his life, but could never wait to get to his 'little summer shack on the beach,' as he called this place. And after two, maybe three holidays here as a tiny child, if vaguely, Kate pictured it as the perfect place for summer holidays, children paddling in the sea, of Rachel. She felt her throat constrict, the memory of her daughter as clear to her as the brightest of summer days.

Telling herself the bungalow needed attention, that grandpa would expect her to smarten it up, probably thought a good clean out the first thing she'd do, perhaps caring for it the sole reason he left the bungalow to her. How he'd slept on that old bunk puzzled Kate, but then, maybe like her, he'd let the ebb and flow of the night tide lull him to sleep. A new bed and second armchair were necessities. The old boy would've accused her of throwing her money about, solemnly reminded her, as he'd done so often in the past, 'If youth could know what age would crave, many a sixpence he would save.'

Yet, at the end of the dear old boy's penny pinching life, the sum total of his estate was this, his April to October home which he swore made the dismal November to March months bearable.

Would the switch to wintering here work equally well for her? She glanced at the bulging shopping bags, told herself to concentrate, think positively and have a decent meal for a change. Stir-fry chicken and vegetables to celebrate an incident that worked in her favour today. Kate lifted the bags off the living room floor.

Nothing earth-shattering, but a conversation with a man, however practical and ordinary was a huge improvement, even if his questioning tactics were less appreciated than his offer to carry this load down the long, lonely road from the village.

He'd seemed perfectly happy to talk simply and quietly about the big, Norfolk skies, the sea, laid stress on the contrariness of winter tides, but primarily and with more enthusiasm on birds of passage.

While there were plenty of tattered papers and magazines on a range of subjects in the bungalow when she arrived, suprisingly, no books til she bought some. Grandpa saving sixpences, she suspected, spreading a lacy, slightly yellowed cloth over the gate-legged table, considering a book on British birds wouldn't come amiss in a place like this.

The next time she was in the village she'd do something about that.

In the stillness of an unusally calm winter evening, the only sound the incoming tide followed by the pull of sea-dragged shingle, until the most unnatural, ear-splitting hammering at her door just about scared Kate out of her wits. 'Whoever you are, I've no intention of opening my door to anyone at this time of night. What do you want?' She shouted angrily.

'It's Mike Tasker, Mrs Ferguson. I've brought you a tide table.'

Relief flooded through her, steadying her jumpy nerves. Opening the door, she apologised. 'Please come in. I'd no idea who it could be.'

'My fault. I should've called out before I knocked. If you're about to have your meal, I've chosen a bad time, but just come off duty.' He grinned. 'It smells good.'

That there was enough for two crossed Kate's mind, but he'd either already eaten or his wife would have his meal ready and waiting for him.

'Your wife would cook something more substantial than pieces of chicken and a few vegetables, I imagine,' she began, hesitantly.

'Chicken and vegetables sound great to me . . . and there's no wife.'

'In that case, if you're hungry and have nothing better to do, you're welcome to pull a chair up to the table.'

'Are you sure there'll be enough for two?'

'More than I could possibly eat,' she replied, hurrying to put the finishing touches to the meal, setting the table for two an unexpectedly gratifying feeling.

Thanking him for the tide table immediately sparked a conversation on freak winds, high tides and the need to be vigilant. 'Especially so for someone living alone at the beach,' Mike added, pointedly.

Mike heard about Kate the day she arrived and since learned she went out of her way to distance herself from others. He wondered why, wanted to ask, but fear of embarrassing her stopped him. A sensible woman, but with no idea of the danger she faced living here at this time of year. Nonetheless, he wished he hadn't frightened her earlier.

The minute Kate went to make coffee, he stole a glance round the sparsely furnished room. Two dining chairs, one well-worn armchair, table and a sideboard. She deserved better than this; looked, dressed and spoke as if accustomed to a hell of a lot better, and he wondered what such a vulnerable young woman was doing here alone. Leaning forward, he took a closer look at the small, silver-framed picture on the sideboard, recognised Kate, but not the pretty little girl or the man.

He took a mug of steaming coffee from her hand. 'Thanks. Would you mind if I called you Kate? And look, I'm sorry for sounding a prophet of doom, but please treat this seriously. If there is any danger, there'll be a flood warning and that's the time to move quickly. You could keep a change of clothing packed and ready for a night in the community centre.'

Horrified, Kate stammered, 'Spend a night, maybe longer in a community centre? I couldn't do that. I go miles out of my way to avoid crowds since the . . . the accident.'

Mike didn't know what to say, neither did he need a shrink to tell him that, whatever the accident was, she'd been through hell and back since. 'If there was a warning,' he began gently, 'you can't stay here.'

'Please don't worry, it would take more than a high tide to scare me.'

'Good God, woman, where've you been. Do you not know about the catastrophic floods here in '53 and '78; the battering this coast took?'

'But even if there was a flood warning, the likelihood of a tragedy on that scale ever happening again must be negligible.'

Mike changed tack when he saw he'd little chance of changing her mind. 'What about The Old Rectory then, that's my place in the village. There's a spare bedroom and I'd be on duty all night if the alarm sounded, so you'd have the place to yourself. Only one snag.' He grinned. 'No chicken and vegetables for your dinner, you'd have to fend for yourself. You'd cope with that?'

'If I were you. Sergeant Tasker, I'd give more thought to such a generous offer. Harbouring the woman on the beach might not be looked on locally as a work of mercy.'

Laughing at her spiky sense of humour, he glanced at his watch. 'Thanks for a most enjoyable meal. I'll help wash this lot up then head home, but before I do,' He dug in his pocket for a bunch of keys, unhooked one and handed it to her. 'For the front door of The Old Rectory if needed.'

On the way to her bedroom, Kate brushed her fingers affectionately over the little picture of Stuart and Rachel, mulling over stern warnings to the uninitiated being part of the police remit in this vicinity, and thanked God no one knew about her bleakest moments when being swallowed by an angry sea sounded the perfect answer to ending the sadness and pain. Thankfully, the blackness was gradually changing to degrees of grey these days, lighter shades she was learning to live with.

Expectantly, she looked for the return of the old Kate. Set herself targets, asked for little, certainly expected less than that joyous, good-to-be-alive surge to happen overnight. But then, a few days ago she'd surprised herself, woke to the sound of the sea and the air filled with squawking birds, had jumped out of bed, pulled on clothes and jogged the length of the beach and back. That was a first and heady stuff when combined with finding the patience to calmly sit and listen to another person, absorbing every word. She'd enjoyed listening to Mike talk about himself. Then making a meal and finding the courage to invite a man to share it really was an unlooked-for improvement; progress beyond her wildest expectations a few weeks ago.

Buying a newspaper in the village the following Friday, Kate overheard a lady customer telling Mr Hedley, as confidentially as a naturally strident voice allowed, that Mike Tasker was in London on an important police course adding, as she leaned across the counter to stress the seriousness of Mike's mission, 'Probably drug related.'

'Funny thing for Mike not to call in and tell me.' Mr Hedley replied, leaving Kate wondering if the newsagent read minds on the side.

'Did he say when he'd be back?'

'In two or three weeks, Mr Hedley, so I was told.'

In the event, six weeks passed before she saw Mike in his favourite spot, binoculars in hand. He waved, slipped and slid towards Kate who stopped to catch her breath after ploughing through a mile-long shelf of wet shingle.

'How're things with you, Kate?'

'Apart from screaming calf muscles, fine. How's life in the big city?'

He gazed at her for a moment, thought she looked more than fine. 'The sea air hasn't done you any harm at all.'

'I feel better, but can't wait to get out of these wet clothes. You're welcome to a hot drink.'

They caught up with the latest news on the way to the bungalow. Mike related some of his more amusing exploits during his stay in town making Kate laugh and wish for an easy way to tell him.

'It's good to hear you laugh, Kate.'

'Since coming here, somewhere along the way, I've found myself, Mike. Can you believe this was the only recourse left to me? I couldn't live in my home another day being continually plagued by memories of the past, external pressures from all sides pressing in on me til I couldn't think straight, finally couldn't think for myself with any clarity. Shock, they said, on the verge of a complete breakdown if I didn't take their advice. I was desperate, Mike, but another memory surfaced, one from my childhood, of sun, sea and this beach bungalow.'

'You were a very unhappy lady, Kate, but not any longer.'

'You're right, I can laugh again. It's time to go back, face my demons and get on with my life.'

'I understand,' he said thoughtfully, 'But keep the key to my place, you never know when it might come in handy.'

'Summertime I thought,' she said with a smile, feeling physically strong enough for the journey home, the innermost journey on hold.

© 2004 Patricia Walton

A GAME OF CHANCE

The car transporter slowed as it neared the service station, the journey from the Coventry manufacturer a temper-testing, bumper to bumper crawl, Matt reflected sourly as he watched Barney manoeuvre the cumbersome vehicle off the road surface to a narrow, tree-lined sliproad with the confident know-how of his twenty years trucking experience.

And as disgruntled as he felt today, he gave Barney his due. When it came to driving big, unwieldy vehicles like this, he was a true professional and a genuine guy who, for some unknown reason, seemed to understand him when so few did.

'There's nothing to hang about here for, Barney. Ten minutes should be enough to water the horses and have a hot drink,' Matt suggested, raising a wrist to look at his watch, muttering an oath, instantly aware Barney had seen the move and no doubt guessed his watch had gone the way of just about everything else he owned. 'Anyway, a few extra minutes in the coffee shop won't hurt; we'll be in Gateshead long before the blizzard hits us.'

Barney burst out laughing. 'For such a young 'un, Matt, you're a right Jeremiah. It's cold enough I grant you, but look at that blue sky. Why man, the sun's ready to break through any minute,' he pointed out, pushing the car door open and lowering himself to slippery tarmac.

After a quick drink, Barney headed for the cash desk while Matt waited, hovering near the smiling blonde in the kiosk, her long, straight hair reminding him of his wife, but Debbie didn't smile a lot these days, and if he was honest, didn't have much to smile about recently. But he was well on the way home to Newcastle and a whole weekend off gave him time to put things right between them.

Barney let Matt walk ahead, preferred to lag behind with his thoughts for company along with a breath of fresh air. Glancing at the sky, he reckoned there was no chance of snow today, that the weathermen had miscalculated royally. It was too cold for snow, other than the usual sprinkling at this time of year on higher ground, the mountain tops further north, the Grampians maybe.

His Rose would worry if the weather turned, her eyes on the clock waiting, getting more nervous by the minute. She considered his job too dangerous, was constantly on at him about taxi drivers and their cushier lifestyle. That said, Rose was always a powerful incentive for him to push on, and when had the pull not been a night in his own bed, his wife's soft, warm body against his. Barney smiled. That was motivation enough for him to get a job finished and head home.

And despite heavy traffic, today's wasn't a bad run, he assessed, his mind on the last cars to be delivered, his eyes, from habit, quickly scanning the load before swinging himself into the cab.

'Another two hours should do it,' he shouted, hoping to be heard above Matt's old country and western tape.

'Yeah, home by teatime,' Matt agreed, his head keeping time to Tammy Wynette belting out D-I-V-O-R-C-E.

Laughing at his young protege, Barney said, 'You sound almost as eager as me to get home.'

Turning down the volume. Matt paused before hesitantly saying, 'Well, Debbie's coming back home today, and we have to make a go of it this time, if only for little Josh's sake. She's given me fair warning, says she's sick and tired of begging money from her family to pay our bills, and swears if she leaves me again, she'll never come back.'

'She's said that a few times,' Barney reminded him.

'You're right, but it's down to me this time. I've reached the stage where I have to accept responsibility for having a wife and bairn, and promised faithfully that I'll stop gambling altogether if she comes back.'

'You were both too young to get married, Matt, that's the trouble.'

'It wasn't a shotgun do, y'know. I know she was pregnant, but I loved Debbie and wanted to marry her.'

'She's a nice lass and if only for her sake, it's time you got your act together. Women'll give a man just so much leeway, and by all accounts, you've overstepped the mark more than once, Matt.'

'This time, Barney, things'll be different. I've turned over a new leaf, decorated the sitting room, painted it her favourite colour, a primrose shade. It looks great and I'm sure she'll like it. The other thing is, I've sworn to her my gambling days are over, that I'll never put a bet on anything, not mention it, even think of it again.'

'Aye, well, you might need a bit of help with a promise like that, Matt. They say it's an addiction like drink or drugs, and some form of counselling's what you need, but to me, whatever handle the so-called experts put on it, throwing hard-earned cash away's a mug's game.'

Glancing at the dashboard clock. Barney saw they were making good time on the motorway. The oil tanker ahead was pressing on at a steady pace, but he was content keeping a safe distance behind.

And he believed Matt's resolution to quit gambling was sincere, didn't doubt his intention to change his ways, just hoped this wasn't another of his pie crust promises, if only for the sake of his long-suffering wife.

It brought to mind his mother's dire warnings to him of how the road to hell was paved. His ma, bless her heart, had an apt adage for all occasions, most of them imprinted on his memory to this day!

'There you are, what did I tell ya,' Matt shouted, cocking a thumb at the spattered windscreen with a smug, sidelong glance at Barney who reluctantly admitted the day had suddenly changed, the sky now uniformly grey with the added nuisance of an unexpected north-easterly picking up.

The wipers had no sooner cleared the windscreen than a barrage of hailstones bombarded the transporter with such speed and force, even the brassy staccato of Matt's tape failed to muffle it's ear-splitting impact.

'A front, that's all this is,' Matt said casually, watching Barney change down to a lower gear, bringing their speed to little more than a crawl.

A few minutes later, the hail storm stopped as quickly as it started, a noisy prelude to the first snow of the year.

Matt and Barney looked at each other and, simultaneously, burst out laughing.

An hour later, it was colder, snowing steadily, beginning to drift, the countryside around them taking on a bleak, polar landscape character, making driving the graceless transporter on a now treacherously slippery road surface, hazardous.

Making it home for tea looked a long shot, Matt mused. And who would believe a day could change so rapidly, but we were warned, and this is exactly what was forecast – with a right vengeance!

'We're barely moving forward, but the tanker ahead's still pressing on regardless,' Barney muttered, assessing the worsening road conditions, anticipating the predictable, yet aware there were always unforeseen problems, knowing from past experience the serious damage weather like this could afflict on a heedless driver.

Nearing Darlington, Barney reckoned it was time to call it a day.

'Visibility's too bad to risk. going any further. Matt. I'm pulling onto the hard shoulder,' he said, automatically sliding a glance in his rear-view mirror, disbelieving his eyes, looked again and shouted despairingly, 'Good God above. There's a guy in a red sports car asking for real trouble here, driving like a maniac and ... I don't believe it, but he is, he's gonna overtake us! What the hell's the half-wit trying to do, kill . . . '

'Never mind him, Barney, the tanker driver's another one in trouble,' Matt cut in, his jaw dropping as he witnessed the tanker skid, jack-knife and slew across the road before coming to a standstill in the path of the sports car heading straight as a bullet for it.

In a cold sweat. Matt saw the car's brake lights, but knew it was too late to do anything other than wait for the inevitable to happen.

'Hold on, Matt,' Barney barked, bringing the transporter to a juddering stop, the deafening impact of the car ploughing into the tanker, sending splittering glass and metal flying off in all directions.

And in that blinding moment, young Matt was confronted for the first time with what he assumed the abrupt end to a man's life.

'Like in the blink of an eye it happened, Barney,' he muttered, more to himself, overwhelmed by the horrendous incident, thinking they were all as vulnerable as the car driver, that if life can end quicker than you can toss a coin in the air, he should be making the most of his instead of worrying about a bit of innocent gambling. One thing for sure, that poor sod's luck had run out – maybe permanently!

Barney glanced at Matt's pale face. 'I've phoned the police. They're on their way. Hey lad, are you feeling alright?'

Matt nodded, the suddenness of the crash staying with him. 'Hell, Barney, what's life but a game of chance, a throw of the dice, win or lose, eh?' He shrugged. 'Tell you what, as much as I hope he makes it, I'd lay odds against the poor bastard walking away from a crash like that,' Matt speculated darkly.

© 2004 Patricia Walton

VAL WILSON

Val Wilson was born in Coventry, and so far no-one has tried to send her back there! She grew up in Worcester, and her happiest memories from this period are of country walks among the abundant wild flowers and orchards full of blossom. She left to go to University in London, and ended up staying there for 12 years, doing jobs ranging from publishing to teaching to a spell in a Japanese travel agency. She moved to rural Norfolk 25 years ago and has been there ever since, except when travelling abroad. Apart from her writing she is a keen photographer and a student of Egyptology.

A RIVER RUNS THROUGH IT

(An ode to the village of Harpley)
It looks over the fields from the top of a hill
A jumble of houses whose graceful old mill
Waits proud at the edge, and stands sentinel still;
And when it rains, a river runs through it.
Water spills out from the lake in the trees
And channels itself down the main street with ease,
Though the flood won't exactly reach up to your knees
When it rains, a river runs through it.
The gardens of Harpley are second to none.
Flowers demure and exotic, flamboyant and unknown
Greet biennial visitors in the warm summer sun,
Or if it rains, a river runs through it.
Past and present find peace in the tranquil churchyard.
Stately stone, mellow green. Flowers and trees, its not hard
Calm and fellowship inside 'neath the angels regard
But outside, when the heavens open, a river runs through it
There is no village green, but right there at the hub
Is the staunchly defended historic old pub
With its picturesque lawn and its fabulous grub,
And when it rains, the river flows past it.
Now we won't mention Back Street where no water flows,
Though there is a fine pond there as everyone knows,
But from new Raven's Yard down to St. Lawrence Close
When it rains, a river runs through it.

© 2004 Val Wilson

FIRST AND ONLY

In all of my life, I have only once spent Christmas away from my home and family. I was about 15, and not only was it the first and only time I have been away from home for Christmas – not only away from home, but abroad – it was also the first time I had flown, and the first and only time I have ever travelled first class.

To explain how this happened, I need to tell you how I met my French penfriend, Françoise. Through my school I booked a place on an organized exchange for children, with accompanied group travel but individual home stays. The form we had to fill in, in order to pair us up with suitable partners, was long and detailed, and I have my own theory as to why Françoise and I were chosen for each other. One of the questions on the form was 'How many rooms are there in your house?', an attempt, I suppose, to unite families of similar wealth and social class. At the time we inhabited one half of a large, crumbling, badly converted Victorian house with four bedrooms. With childish literalness I counted not only all of these, and the other principal rooms, but also the cellars, of which there were four, and probably the hallway and pantry too. Françoise, whose mother and sister were midwives, lived in a private maternity clinic owned by her family, and I have always suspected that she counted not only the rooms of the downstairs flat where they lived, but also all the bedrooms upstairs which were occupied by pregnant ladies!

Whether this is true or not, the pairing system seems to have worked, as Françoise and I got on like a house on fire. So much so, that at Easter the following year, keen to improve her English, she invited herself back, suggesting I should visit her in the summer. Unfortunately, I had made other arrangements, but we said we would be delighted to receive Françoise at Easter anyway, without charge and with no obligation for a return visit, and so we did. Such an obligation must have weighed upon her family, however, as in the Autumn they wrote inviting me to visit them for Christmas at Juvisy, near Paris, where they lived, suggesting that as the Christmas holidays were shorter than the Easter ones, they should also pay my air fare. The first class ticket which later arrived was an added bonus.

And so, one frosty winter's morning in late December, I set off, escorted by my mother, to Birmingham airport for my maiden flight. I still have two greyish monochrome photos of clouds seen from above. I remember the thrill of first take-off and landing, and – just as exciting at the age of fifteen – my first pre-packaged in-flight meal with plastic knives and forks and individual salt and pepper.

What happens at Christmas in France? Well, I arrived several days before the main event, so my first memories are of last-minute Christmas shopping. We went to the local shops in Juvisy, and were pursued by a street photographer. Somewhere I still have the most awful photo of me, with my eyes shut, being cuddled by a French Father Christmas. We also went into central Paris, and I marvelled at the vast array of goods on offer at a seasonally decorated Galeries Lafayette. Outside, on the icy pavements, I learnt a new word, 'gaufre', a kind of waffle on offer from various street vendors. Of course Maman bought some for Françoise and me, and we scattered the powdered sugar with which they were coated everywhere, and got thoroughly and enjoyably sticky.

Another day we went Christmas shopping with Papa, but on a very specific mission, to choose Maman's Christmas present. We went to Paris again, but not this time to the glittering public shops. No, we went to one of those mellow, ancient buildings which abound in France, with a creaking, old-fashioned lift. When we alighted from it however, we were faced with a door with several very modern locks, and an entry-phone through which we were only allowed to pass after careful scrutiny from inside And here comes another 'first and only' – the first and only time I have been inside a Paris diamond merchant's and had trays and trays of diamonds laid out before me for my personal scrutiny. Papa, of course was the one who made the final choice of gem, since he was paying for it.

On Christmas Eve, Françoise and I had a special task to perform. Like busy mothers the world over, Maman had no doubt thought to herself 'Let's give one of the really easy jobs to the children to do, it will keep them occupied'. Well, it was a task we performed without grumbling, I can tell you. What did we have to do? We had to make the chocolate truffles which are a Christmas tradition over there. We mixed them and rolled them into balls, and coated them in cocoa powder, and I could hardly wait to eat them. In fact, I didn't have to wait too long. We stayed up very late, in order to go to the Midnight Mass at the large white modern church in Juvisy, and it seemed very strange to me to be walking through the streets at that hour, chatting to the friends and neighbours. After the Service we came back home, and the truffles formed part of the feast that we had.

What happened on Christmas day? Do you know, I don't remember a thing! There must have been presents, but I've no idea what they were. The French make rather less of Christmas and more of New Year than we do, and in the intervening period they send out cards and entertain and are entertained by family and friends. Of course, as a guest I went along to all these visits and communal meals, and this gave rise to the only slightly unhappy memory of the holiday. One house we visited was splendid, but rather dark and chilly. The family were very formal, and obviously well-off. We sat down at a long table and were presented with the first course, no doubt at great expense and designed to impress. It was greeted rapturously by all the other diners. In front of each person, including myself, stood a dish piled high with a dozen raw oysters. I have never eaten a raw oyster, The idea does not appeal to me. One, maybe, I could have coped with. I am not unadventurous. Françoise and maman had introduced me to snails the year before. But a dozen? I politely declined, on the grounds that if I hadn't touched them at all they could be given to some-one else, but I felt uncomfortable for the rest of the meal.

Back at the maternity clinic again, I quickly settled down and enjoyed the rest of my visit. Françoise and I were occasionally allowed to visit the upper regions, and it was there that I finally understood the Christmas phrase 'They wrapped him in swaddling clothes.' Here is another (first and only) – this was the first and only time I have ever seen a baby swaddled. It was the custom at this clinic to bind the new born babies quite tightly with lots and lots of bandages so that they could not move, forming a handy package which could easily be passed from one to another. Seriously though, I don't know why this custom was practised or whether it is still current.

Finally, it was time for me to go home. Simple, you might think. I had my ticket with my comfortable first-class reserved seat. But no, on the day of departure the family telephoned the airport and announced to me 'Birmingham airport is snowed up. Either you must fly to Manchester and return to Birmingham by train, or you must wait until it is clear'. Fortunately, much as I had enjoyed my stay in France, I decided not to wait. The next day, Manchester was also snowed up and I would have had to fly to Edinburgh.

It was a wonderful flight, for a novice like me. Two hours in the air, instead of one, and the most wonderful views as we approached the runway, dropping down below the clouds and coming in long and low. Everywhere was covered in white as we skimmed over little Christmas card villages with a central church and lots of little houses with the lights spilling out onto the snow. After we landed I was given my ticket to get me home to Birmingham – the first and only time I have ever travelled in a first class railway carriage.

© 2004 Val Wilson

THE GUNMAN IN THE HEDGE

Many is the night I have walked the dog along this particular lane. In summer, it is often possible to fit in his last outing during the hours of daylight without the risk of finding a nasty surprise on the carpet next morning, but in winter we are always out after dark. You might think I would be a little nervous, alone, but all the little country noises, the squeaks and rustles in the hedge, even the weird call of some unidentified night-bird are so familiar now that they no longer seem creepy to me. No, the strangest, the scariest, the most unsettling experience I ever had happened when I had company.

One night, my daughter decided to come with me. We were chatting amicably when she suddenly stopped, put a restraining hand on my arm, and whispered nervously 'There's a man with a gun'.

I looked where she was looking, towards the hedge. A faint moonglow showed a network of twigs interspersed with deep patches of shadow. I probed the shadows for a figure, but saw none. 'Where?' I whispered back.

She described the exact point in the hedge where he stood. 'Can't you see him?' she asked.

'No' I said. I went closer to the hedge. She hung back, terrified. If there are hairs on the back of my neck, they were definitely standing on end.

It was the strangest feeling, being with some-one who was convinced they could see something I could not see. I gazed intently into every dark shadow, even those far too small to conceal a person, I ventured a hesitant 'Good evening' and got no response. I bombarded myself with logic, telling myself that no-one would squeeze himself into the middle of a close knit hedge. My eyes convinced me there was no-one there, but my daughter's conviction filled me with alarm. Finally though, we were, as I thought, reassured, and continued on our way home, quickly gaining the security of our warm, well-lit house.

Much later – weeks later I spoke to my daughter again about the incident. She is still convinced there was a gunman in the hedge.

© 2004 Val Wilson

RESURRECTION

I have stopped screaming now. I gaze down at my bandaged hands, which still ache a little, lying on the white sheet. The doctor says I am fit to travel, I can go home tomorrow. The holiday will be over, the holiday which I hoped would revive my spirits and enable me to live again. In a way it has been successful, although this did not come about at all as I expected when I arrived here a little over a week ago.

The sun shone brightly on the bright flowers in the garden which sloped down to the river beside the great cathedral. The sun was still hot, although it was nearly 5 o'clock in the afternoon, but its warmth did not reach my broken heart. I stepped through the arched doorway into the cool interior of the great church, whose dim shadows and cold stone floor better fitted my melancholy mood.

I saw the fateful sign almost at once, though I paused to admire my surroundings before making my way towards it. The carved stonework was magnificent, the vaulted roof soared upwards toward heaven. Here and there a golden shaft of light touched a gilded king or an intricate stone carving, or passed through a stained glass window and splashed onto the floor in a shower of sparkling jewels. However, I had come to see the crypt, which was supposed to be especially wondrous, and I turned now towards the sign marking its entrance. The sign informed me that it would be closing in a few minutes, so I hurried forward. I felt not the slightest sense of foreboding.

Steep stone steps led down to a subterranean world of graceful vaults and columns. At the top of each vault was a carved stone boss, each one different – a flower, a bunch of leaves, a creature of some kind. Angels flew overhead, even here below ground, but they were vastly outnumbered by beings which could only have come from the netherworld.

There was one other visitor, a young man whose pale skin matched the polished stonework of the pillar by which he stood. He ran his slender finger over its smooth surface without disturbing the film of moisture which covered it. I gazed at him. He was beautiful. There was no other word for it, beautiful with the delicate grace of the carved stonework which surrounded us, and which, because the columns were not perfectly aligned but appeared always in between each other, between and between, on into the distance, seemed to have no end. He turned his beautiful dark eyes towards me, and immediately a link was formed. I felt as if I would burst if I did not share the wonder of this place with some-one.

"Isn't it exquisite?" I exclaimed.

"You like this place?" he asked.

"Oh, yes" I breathed.

His voice was strange, it had a flatness about it "It is a place for dead people" he said.

The reply seemed to come from far away, although I was drawn towards this man as if mesmerised and now stood so close that I could easily touch him.

"There are no dead people here now," I said, looking at the walls which surrounded us. There were niches and shelves but the coffins had gone long ago.

"I'm alive" I added, although even as I said the words I was not sure if they were entirely true. I felt as if I had died two years ago. My heart, as if encased in a block of ice, had refused to feel anything since that time, since it could not bear the pain of separation.

"There is no pain here" said the young man, as if I had spoken aloud. "It is so peaceful, don't you think?" He was smiling now, almost tenderly. Once again, I felt drawn to him. He reached out to touch me with that pale hand, and I held out my own hand to grasp his slender fingers. Cold, so cold. It was like touching the hand of a marble statue. I felt the heat draining from my own body, but suddenly the bond was broken. A flood of light engulfed us, a harsh voice shattered the silence, calling out from the top of the staircase: "We are closed. Will all visitors please make there way to the exit?". Galvanised by these words, I staggered up the stone steps, dazed and blinking as if I had been rudely awakened from a deep sleep.

I emerged into the sunlight, which was still bright, and felt its warmth on my skin. I stood, disorientated for a moment, then looked around for my erstwhile companion. He was nowhere to be seen. In fact, the church was now completely empty, since the custodian seemed to have disappeared also. As I stood there, the light suddenly dimmed – a cloud must have passed over the face of the sun – and the air grew cold. A brighter light was still visible through the open doorway, and I hastened towards it. Outside in the garden it was still warm. Bees hummed gently among the flowers, with whose scent the air was laden. Life coursed through my veins again, and I welcomed it.

That night, there was a festival in the piazza. There were bright lights, there was music and dancing. I danced, I got a little drunk, and I told myself it did not matter that my soul had no companion, since I had friends to share this holiday with, and I was having a wonderful time. We laughed and sang together, and grew very close, and as we finally made our way back to the hotel a warm glow surrounded me.

Why then, on the morrow, did I feel compelled to go back to the cathedral? Had I not already felt a slight sense of unease, of something not quite natural? I know that I had, and yet I felt something irresistibly pulling me back. I told myself that I simply wanted to admire the beauties of the famous crypt at leisure, in a relaxed and unhurried way, with no constraints of time. And yet I dawdled along my way, looking in shop windows, visiting an exhibition en route, stopping to feed the pigeons in the piazza, sitting down at a cafe and sipping freshly squeezed orange juice from a chilled glass, so that it was already four o'clock when I once again stepped through the doorway into the vast cathedral.

This time, the beautiful young man was standing in the main part of the church, admiring an elegantly carved pillar. He immediately turned towards me and smiled, even though he was some distance away, and I was not aware of having made any sound as I came in. The original sense of attraction had returned, and I felt no strangeness any more. We moved towards each other.

"You came back" he said.

"Yes" I said "So did you".

He did not reply. Instead he began to talk to me of the many wonders of the great church, which he seemed to know in minute detail. As a keen student of both architecture and history, I was fascinated by everything he had to say, and the bond between us grew. His knowledge of history, in particular, was extensive and detailed, and he talked of those who lived in times past with a vividness which almost seemed to make them live again.

We arrived at the top of the steps which led down to the crypt. "Do you want to come in?" he asked, almost as if he was inviting me into his abode – which of course he was, and in my heart I knew it, although I had not fully realised it then. We descended the stone staircase and entered once more the maze of graceful pillars, the world of soaring angels and leering devils, of pale polished marble and ice-cold stone. I was enchanted. I felt the coldness of his hand in mine, and the icy coldness of his lips on mine, and it was what I wanted. Oblivion. Release. Very faintly, as if from a great distance, the voice of the custodian announced that it was closing time. A moment later the door at the top of the staircase slammed shut, and the crypt was plunged into total darkness. I felt the last vestiges of warmth draining from my body as I stood there, unable to move or speak clasped in the embrace of some creature from beyond the grave as I descended into hell. Vile monsters surrounded me, slimy and stinking. Dead eyes stared at me, dead hands pawed and clawed at me, trying to drain the life from me, and suddenly that life seemed more important than anything. I remember finding one tiny little point of light, somewhere deep inside myself and focusing on it, and refusing to let go. But there wasn't any light really, not until they opened the door, and by then I was already at the top of the steps, not knowing how I got there, my fists, my knees, my feet, even my forehead torn and bloodied where I had battered myself against the unyielding woodwork with every ounce of strength I possessed. As the heavy door swung open and let in the sunlight, I could hear myself screaming very loudly.

© 2004 Val Wilson

COLLABORATION

Adorable Dora admired herself: gorgeous dress, perfect fit – hateful necklace (hubby's pride.) She sniffed. £500,000 insurance money would buy so many more flattering trinkets.

Barely respectable Reg dressed smartish. Must blend with the crowd.

Limousine draws up, glimpse of svelte leg, flashing emeralds. Dora alights. Engulfed by milling theatregoers she looks carefully away from the seedy chap with intense eyes, pauses, fiddles with her handbag until she feels the faintest tug.

Christmas presents after all, gloats Reg. I've waited years. It's pay-off time.

Dora draws her glamorous stole closer round her neck. She glows without gems. Nobody notices anything amiss.

© 2004 Val Wilson

REVERIE

The magic wood spread out before me as I sat on the familiar lawn, half dozing in my deckchair in the warm sun of late afternoon. The trees crept right up to the edge of the grass – there was no fence – and stretched out a hundred arms, beckoning. I imagined myself springing upright from the chair, gliding over the surface of the lawn, and drifting off among them, lost in a world of green and gold. But no, not any more. It was too late now. I was too old.

As a child, this had been my home. It had been my parents' house. Now my daughter lived here, with her family, and although I visited often, it was quite a while since I had sat out in the garden on a late summer's afternoon. The pleasure I would have felt normally was today tinged with sadness. A pall of melancholy and unnatural silence hung over this grief stricken household which mourned the loss of its master – young Andrew, my son-in-law, only twenty-nine years old, killed in a car crash.

A week had passed, but the shock and numbness had not. The funeral was over, Anne and the children had cried their eyes out until they stopped from sheer exhaustion, and then started again. And now, this awful quiet, where the shouts and laughter of playing children should be. Little James sat beside me on the grass, a tiny, stiff, upright figure, not making a sound but following my every movement with his eyes. He had seen me looking intently towards the wood, and his intent gaze had followed mine. Then he turned and looked at me, with big eyes, and said "Do you know how to fly?" My heart stopped for a moment. I knew what he meant, but I didn't want to know. That was all over so very long ago. There was no going back now. So I mumbled things about having been up in aeroplanes, but not actually being able to pilot one, and left it at that. He didn't push it, but I felt he had an idea that I was avoiding the issue.

Jess. My sister, Jess. No-one had told me that I had had a sister. She had died when she was three, just after I was born. I was four when I found the secret path in the wood, and no-one had told me about her yet. The chicken-pox had struck me down, made me feverish and slightly delirious, and kept me in bed for a week. Mum and Dad coddled and cosseted me, brought me meals and lots of drinks, filled my hot water bottle, and read me stories, but time passes terribly slowly when you're that little, and the intervals between their visits to my room seemed interminable. I spent a lot of time alone, hovering on the edge of sleep, but wakeful. In this half-dreaming state I would float up from my bed and drift around the room, bumping against the ceiling, and looking down at the rumpled bedclothes and the glass of water on my bedside table.

It was a late summer afternoon. Mum had taken my tea-tray away, and I was half asleep, drifting, drifting. The weather was very hot, the window was open, my feet were on the sill, and I was looking down at the lawn. Fear was a long way away as I launched myself into space, buoyed up by a cushion of air, descending gently to the grass below. My feet never touched the ground, I glided across the lawn on some kind of air current which drew me towards the trees. Fending them off on either side, like going through a tunnel in a boat, I let the current steer me along the pathways, through sunlit glades and darker shadows where the branches met completely overhead. It slowed gradually until my feet did at last touch the ground, and I was walking.

Walking along a path which I didn't recognise. And then I saw her, a little girl of about three, with bright golden curls and a smile full of joy.

"I'm so glad you've come at last," she said, and threw her arms around me and hugged me.

"Who are you?" I asked.

"I'm your sister, Jess." she said.

"I don't have a sister," I said.

"Yes you do," she said. "Come and play with me."

So we played together among the trees: Hide and seek and chasing games, and 'I spy' until we got tired. I felt puzzled, but I was only little, remember. The whole of life was a puzzle, and if you asked too many questions people always got cross. It wouldn't do to make Jess cross, she was fun to be with.

As the shadows started to lengthen, she seemed to become

uneasy.

"You should go," she said, glancing at the setting sun. "Come again soon".

She held out her hand I took it, and she led me back through the maze of greenery till we reached the edge of the lawn. There she stopped, and I went on, running faster and faster over the grass until I took a giant leap into the air and propelled myself back through the open window of my room. Turning back towards the wood I stared and probed its shadows for some time but Jess was gone. I left the window and lay down on my bed, where I fell asleep.

The chicken-pox went away at last, and I was allowed downstairs again. I had stood at the window many times, but never again dared to jump. It didn't seem possible, it was much too far down. Everything that had happened seemed like a dream, probably was a dream. I said nothing to my parents, and when I went to play in the wood none of the paths looked like the one I had followed that day. Then, when I was seven, they told me about Jess. Yes, her name was Jess, she had died of pneumonia when she was three, she had golden, curly hair, and her favourite game was 'I spy'. Why didn't I tell them that I already knew that? I don't know.

Another week passed. Anne was starting to slip back into her routine – shopping housework, seeing her friends again. Soon, I would be able to go home, they would be able to manage without me. Little James had had a couple of mates round for a very energetic game of football all over the lawn, and had gone to bed early, tired out It was a hot, drowsy, late summer afternoon, as I relaxed in my deckchair and stared up at the bedroom window. It was open. James stood there looking down at me. Our eyes met as he leapt into space and drifted down towards the lawn. I caught his hand as he glided past me, and was drawn along with him towards the wood.

The path was familiar. Jess stood where she had stood before, her golden hair glowing in the sunlight. She saw me, ran towards me, and hurled herself into my arms. Beyond her, slightly more in shadow, stood a man. He turned, it was Andrew. Little James pulled his hand away from mine and ran to him. I saw Andrew stroke the boy's hair and speak words of comfort to him. Jess looked up at me. "You've grown big" she said.

"Yes", I said, "How did you know me?"

She smiled at me "When you were born", she said "I was so, so happy. Our souls touched. You were too young to remember, but I shall always know you".

We sat together on the grass in a pool of sunlight and watched a million tiny flying insects dancing up and down the light shafts which slanted down from the leafy canopy overhead. The whole wood hummed gently. Yes, I was big now, too big to play hide and seek. So we just sat there, side by side, and our souls held hands. How long we sat there, I don t know. After a few seconds, or an eternity of time, Jess began to seem more and more restless. She kept looking down the path along which I had come It was darker back there, a strange seething kind of darkness, which somehow made the shapes of the trees indistinct, not quite in focus. The sun was low in the sky. It was getting darker, certainly, but here where we sat the sunlight was still bright. Over there a greyness was spreading everywhere.

Jess stood up and urged me to my feet. She looked at me anxiously "It isn't time for you to stay yet, is it?" she asked. "It's too soon, isn't it?" I felt her tugging me towards the path, but I looked the other way. James' face was buried in Andrew's chest. Andrew sat staring straight ahead, with the little boy on his knees. "Andrew" I called softly, "I think it's time for James to go home." The man looked sad, he didn't have that glow which always surrounded Jess. He got up slowly and led James by the hand towards us. My hand was being tugged ever more insistently, as Jess led the way towards where the path had been, and now a swirling mass of blackness was.

"It's too late" said Andrew.

"No!" said Jess firmly, "They have to go back."

Father and son held each other tight for a moment, then Andrew pressed a final kiss, like a blessing, on James' forehead. He put the little boy's hand in mine, and the two of us turned away from him and followed Jess into the darkness. There was no path, there were no trees. Shreds of grey mist seemed to cling to me tangibly, dragging me back. The darkness was like treacle, sticking to me, slowing me, covering my eyes, blocking my nose till felt I couldn't breathe. I held my breath and forced my legs to work, Jess's hand always pulling me onwards, James holding me back, though I refused to let go of him. It seemed as if my head would burst, and I was on the point of losing consciousness when gradually the resistance seemed to get less, and then less, until at last I could see the lawn, though dimly, as if through a haze of soot. James was exhausted. I picked him up and ran with him out into the brightness of the setting sun, taking deep grateful breaths as I ran. As we reached the middle of the lawn, he seemed to grow lighter and lighter, until he floated out of my arms and drifted up and in through the bedroom window, which was still open.

The late afternoon sun cast long shadows as I stood there on the lawn. Little James looked out through his open bedroom window. He didn't see me. He was gazing wistfully towards the wood.

The next day nothing was said between us, but James seemed calmer and happier than he had been, and we played together on the lawn instead of sitting in silence A new closeness had developed between me and my grandson. He confided in me one day when no-one else was listening.

He said, "I will see Dad again one day, won't I? When its time?"

"Of course you will", I said, and I knew it was alright now for me to go home

© 2004 Val Wilson

CRYSTALLINE

Icicles stabbing downward from the eaves
Spreading upon the windowpane frost trees
Snowflakes briefly caught on Autumn leaves
The sparkling sapphire swell of summer seas
Coarse crumbling salt and granulated sugar
Golden topaz honey too long jarred
Accidentally crunchy frozen yoghourt
Sparkling jewelled jelly that's set hard
Purity chiming, wakened by the wind
Celestial trilling of a mastered flute
The splash of leaping salmon, silver skinned
A proffered diamond's hopeful message mute
A vision glows within that mystic sphere
Where nought is ever hidden from the seer

© 2004 Val Wilson

TENTACLES

I waken to the early morning sun.
Not alone.
Lying beside me there is one
Who is my own. For always.
I enfold him with my gaze,
no need to touch, so many days
we've loved already, and so many ways
we've promised to remain in love. For always.
The tentacles of my hearing stretch out now.
Baby's there.
The bedside speaker tells me how
He takes in air. Steadily.
Not-quite-baby moves about,
I think I heard a little shout,
Yes! Eldest child is coming out,
The sun is up, she's getting up. Readily.
My mind has tentacles too, which reach,
some long, some short,
with eager, loving grasp to each
and all I know and need.
Cut one, I'd hurt and heal, though scarred.
To sever all would be too hard.
If contacts were forever barred
I'd shrivel and be dead indeed.

© 2004 Val Wilson

SOUL-CLAMPED

The rigid metal chair stands on the seafront,
Its brake-clamped wheels held motionless
There on the promenade

The legless warrior leaps down the stone steps to the beach, races across the sand,
Arms swinging,
Legs springing,
Chest muscles firm and hard.

Bouncing beachball butted back to playing, laughing children.
Toes tingle to that first thrilling, chilling touch of the sea's edge.
Wet sand trickles between them as they dabble and paddle
Splish,
Flash,
Sunlight sparkling on the water.
Deep green.
Deep down.
Emerald seaweed swaying green,
Fish darting,
Scurrying crabs,
Lobster peering with tiny bead-eyes from grey rock crevice.
Fish swimming.
Swimming with fish,
No gills, need air, can't breathe, make for the surface,
Gasping, choking, spluttering.
Lungs fill gratefully with fresh sea-air.
Inhale deeply,
Deeply,
Steady now.

Warm sun blazes down from the deep blue summer sky.
It heats his smooth, tanned back as he stretches out comfortably on the warm sand,

Hollowing out a spot for his knees and elbows.
A breeze skims the surface of his skin.
Sand sticks to it like a light dusting of pepper.
The hairs on his head stir gently as he sinks into sleep.

Harsh seagull cries break into his dream.
A bird alights for a moment beside him,
Then soars aloft.
He flies with it, gliding on tight, white outstretched wings,
Riding the breeze,
Higher and higher,
Bright sea spread out blue below,
To infinite horizons,
Like a limitless treasure trove of shifting sapphires.

The legless, wingless, finless prisoner of the rigid metal chair sits
        on the seafront,
Brake clamped, soul-clamped, motionless, there on the
        promenade.

© 2004 Val Wilson

ROCK BOTTOM

With my marriage on the rocks after 23 years, I decided it was time to become a rock myself. Yes, I was going to change into a rock for the summer.

As it happened, my daughter and her friend, Ros, were about to audition for a local production of 'The Tempest'. Most of the main parts were played by professionals, and those competing for the lesser roles were mostly teenagers, but what the hell. My friend, Maureen (also divorced) and I decided to go along too. Ros was lucky enough to be cast as Miranda, and Maureen, my daughter and I won parts as Ariel's spirits. Our dreams of tripping lightly around in costumes of floaty gauze were soon dashed, however. We were to be dressed as rocks! Can you imagine it? A rock costume? The mind boggled.

The production was to be set in the open air, on a stage constructed in front of a local ruin. We were to be nature spirits, blending in with the background of grey stone. We couldn't believe it. But sure enough, in due course we were all issued with a long-sleeved, hooded top and matching trousers, covered with lumps of polystyrene and skilfully painted.

Soon rehearsals started in earnest. We had to groan and wail in the shipwreck scene, bending and swaying like trees in the wind. We were barking, howling dogs chasing Trinculo, Stephano and the deformed Caliban, we were high-stepping waiters presenting our platters at a grotesque banquet, we were a leafy curtain which parted to reveal the lovers in the final scene. We chanted, sighed and moaned mysteriously, and when the action did not call for our services, we crouched or knelt close to a real rock, and 'disappeared'.

The only problem, as Maureen and I soon discovered, is that middle-aged knees do not bend and crouch for ten minutes at a time as easily as do younger ones. Poor Andy, the director, was very patient with us, until at last we achieved positions where we could be comfortable and didn't wobble. He is a great perfectionist, is Andy, and two wobbly rocks would have completely ruined the desired effect. Sometimes, though, even his patience wore thin as one of us missed a rehearsal, missed a cue, ended up in the wrong spot, or completely forgot what we were supposed to be doing. Would we ever be ready?

Probably not, not completely. But the great day came anyway, at last. It was the night of the first performance. Now we had to wear not only rock costumes, but rock make-up as well – streaks of black, white and grey all over our faces and hands. We crept on to the stage, one by one, and 'blended in', as the audience took their seats. Of course, they saw us come, but there were ten of us altogether, and by the time all of us were in place they couldn't remember where everyone was. The illusion was complete. We could feel the ripple of astonishment as we all leapt to our feet at the beginning of the shipwreck scene. It was a good start, but our hearts were in our mouths. Would we remember everything? By the time we reached the interval, nothing had gone wrong, but our nerves were in shreds. Mike made us coffee to calm us down. We drank it gratefully backstage, that is, behind the tall grey wall of the ruined priory which we were using as a backdrop. Bats fluttered overhead, and cows gazed at us mournfully from the other side of a stream which the monks of old must have used as a water supply. It was very atmospheric.

Our break was all too short, and it was back onstage to crouch beside our rocks. Ariel's theme music floated eerily forth from the loudspeakers, and we were into the second half. Again, nothing went wrong, and we barked, swayed, hissed and chanted our way to a successful conclusion. Andy was pleased with us, and the audience applauded rapturously. Now the only question was, could we do it again?

Apparently we could. Seven more times, in fact. Of course, there were minor hitches, like the time I forgot to put make-up on my hands, or the night it rained and ten soggy spirits dripped their way back to the dressing room with black and white streaks running down their faces, but always we made it to the end. and always the spectators clapped with enthusiasm.

On the last night there was a pre-performance banquet for the audience, and at the end, after Prospero's final speech, all the members of the cast gathered to eat up the leftovers during a hilarious end of season party. And then it was all over, and there was that gap in my life again.

Still, since then Maureen and I have begun meeting regularly with Sarah, another divorcee and the only other rock over 21. Our girls' days out look set to become a regular thing, so my life has at least one new dimension. I wonder what play they're putting on next summer? Will there be a part in it for me, I wonder?

© 2004 Val Wilson

ON DEVOLUTION

At school they taught her to speak French.

Later, she made many French friends.

One of them taught her a French rhyme, to test the power of love by counting the petals of the pretty Marguerite.

She shared the rhyme with an Arab boy, who had learnt French too, as they picked the white flowers together beneath the golden sun of Spain.

Did he love her a little, a lot, or passionately?

They watched the little white petals fall, but that was not, in the end, how they discovered the answer to the question.

Then she learnt Italian, and hitch-hiked with a girlfriend all the way from Milan to Sorrento, and back. They discovered that Italian men judge a woman by the beauty of her teeth, and that Italian communists will let you ride in their car for fourteen hours, or more, as long as you discuss politics all the way (in Italian of course).

At last, she learnt Greek, a little, and told the ages of her daughters to the peasant who offered her an orange from a tree as she strolled in the groves of Olympus. He showed her the olive trees which his family had owned for generations. She shared her lunch with him.

And now, they expect her to understand why the family of her Scottish grandmother will henceforth consider her a foreigner.

© 2004 Val Wilson

RURAL AUTUMN

Cornflakes on the grass
Blonde skinhead fields
Steaming manure piled up like school meals
Mud like chocolate pud
– doesn't taste as good!
The sun sets into a sea of tomato soup.

Aliens prowl the fields at night
Their light-sabres flash in the air as they move to and fro,
And gunshots can be heard as they come and go
Killing all the rabbits in sight.

The early morning fog is torn apart by a flashing-eyed monster
Only a tractor
Now its gone
I'm all alone

Surrounded by grey skeletons with wet brown leaves hanging
    from their bones
Like remnants of dead flesh.
Ghostly figures draped in a tattered shroud of mist, which drifts
    away
As a bright golden football bounces over the horizon.

© 2004 Val Wilson

WETLAND MISCELLANY

Blue water under bluer skies.
Brown water blending with the mud.
Flat water, smooth and limitless.
Flood water lapping round the feet of trees.
Invading water, relentlessly rising, creeping over roads.
Inviting water, sparkling in the sunlight.
Supportive water, bearing flotsam ducks and swans.
Stinking water, caught in puddles, cut off from the flow.
Reflective water, sky on earth, full of moving clouds and flying
   birds.
Red water, sunset's dying glow, as gold and orange fade and
   deepen.
Flowing water carrying pleasure boats, and the occasional
   dredger.
Fleeing water, twisting and turning through myriad channels
   before escaping at last to the sea.
Calm water, steely and unmoving upon the flat fen.
Crying water with swollen-lidded eyes, struggling to escape its
   groaning banks.
Stormy water, blowing white-flecked in the wind.
Silent water, polished black and silver in the moonlight.
Water, water everywhere, dividing the land, consuming the land.
Waterworld, empty yet not empty, place of solitude and peace.

© 2004 Val Wilson

SITTING WITH STELLA

If that Friday hadn't been the day before I set off on a two-week holiday to Kos, I probably would have heard about what happened to Stella. The entire office-block would have been buzzing with the sad news on the following Monday morning. But by the time I got back to work, two weeks later, it had long blown over, and no-one thought to mention it to me.

It was a big company. Stella and I did not interact at all, workwise, and our offices were nowhere near each other. She was a typist – in accounts somewhere, I think -and no-one knew much about her except the people who worked right next to her. Certainly, no-one suspected I knew her, because I didn't. At least, I had never spoken to her. But she taught me to smile at her, to begin to want to know her, to wonder what lay behind that shy smile of hers with which she greeted me each time our paths crossed in the long corridors or the hallway. At first it was a fleeting smile, with eyes quickly averted as she sensed no response from me. Then, as I began to smile at her in return it became ever more radiant, her eyes brimmed with hope, words of reply formed almost visibly on her lips – reply to a spoken greeting which I never ever gave her.

But on that fateful Friday I made her an unspoken promise, and as quickly broke it. It was lunchtime. I had taken my sandwiches to the Park, as usual, and was looking for somewhere to sit. I saw Stella just ahead of me, sitting alone on a bench. Her face broke into a smile of pure delight at the sight of me, she moved along the bench to make room for me, although there was plenty of space already, and smiling myself I quickened my step and steered directly towards her, with the clear and obvious intention of sitting down beside her. Then I heard a shout. Some friends from my own office were picnicking on the grass nearby, had spotted me, and were calling my name. I allowed myself to be distracted, gave Stella a perfunctory wave as if I had never had any other intention, and changed course. I sat on the grass with my back to her in an attempt to disguise a slight feeling of guilt which was, I assured myself, completely unjustified.

On my return from Kos, work proceeded exactly as normal. I handed round my snapshots of sunlit beaches and unbelievably blue sea, but it was as if those places had never existed. The office routine took over my life once more. If I didn't see Stella for the first few days I thought nothing of it, for in fact I never thought of Stella at all except when she smiled at me in passing. It was not until Friday that I saw her, when I took my sandwiches over to the Park.

She was sitting on a bench, and I instantly resolved to make amends for what I felt she might perceive as my previous snub. The bench where she was sitting was some distance away, but I was sure it was her, so I pursued a tortuous route around groups of picnickers, dog walkers, and children playing ball, until I suddenly realised that the bench I was headed for was now empty. Puzzled, since I had not taken my eyes off it for more than a second, I scanned the surrounding area for a walking figure with the familiar downcast eyes and demure dress. There was none, but I quickly spotted Stella again, sitting on another bench, quite far ahead. How could she have had time to walk so far? I supposed that in my efforts to avoid sprawling lunchers and unpredictable canines I must have taken my eyes from the bench for longer than I thought, and steered seriously off course.

Obviously the bench where Stella was sitting was the one where she had been the whole time. I headed towards it, treading a careful path and keeping my eyes firmly fixed on her, until a stray football made contact with my leg and forced me to look down. When I looked up the bench was empty, but when I looked round I could see a figure resembling Stella sitting on another bench right over the far side of the Park. I broke into a run. I was halfway across the intervening space when I realised I was running towards a bench which was completely empty. I was breathless, sweating, time was running out, and I still hadn't eaten my sandwiches. I told myself to get a grip, and turned back towards the office, munching as I went.

I tried to push the incident out of my thoughts, but I couldn't stop myself looking around at work for Stella. I never saw her. I didn't know then of course, that her name was Stella, or exactly which office she worked in, so I couldn't ask anyone if they knew where she was. She didn't seem to be in the Park at lunchtime any more, either. At least, not until Friday, when I spotted her once more. She was on the same bench as before, in fact now I thought about it, it was the same one where I had meant to sit by her on the Friday before my holiday. She disappeared again before I reached her, and I tracked her across the Park, just as I had the previous week. I arrived back at the office seriously disturbed, and with indigestion.

I tried to find out who she was, but she wasn't an easy person to describe. Pleasant, but not particularly pretty, dressed in the manner of the conscientious office worker, in clothes neither fashionable nor unfashionable, neat but not distinctive. In desperation I even made a fool of myself by asking about 'that girl who used to smile at me in the corridor', but no-one else had ever noticed.

The next Friday, I headed straight for the bench on the far side of the Park. This was the side furthest from the offices, and the grass was more or less empty. A fast dual carriageway ran past it, and there were blocks of flats on the far side. Stella was sitting on the bench. She turned towards me, but she did not smile. Her eyes were dark wells of unhappiness. She turned her head again and got up, running away from me and out of the Park gate. My heart froze as I heard a screech of brakes. There was a sickening thud, a grating of metal on stone, a shattering of glass. I raced through the gate and out onto the roadway. There was nothing. No crashed vehicle, no broken glass, no still figure lying there. The busy flow of traffic continued uninterrupted. Not knowing what else to do I turned away and hurried back to work

When I started asking about the accident, of course, there wasn't a single person in the office who couldn't tell me about Stella. How she had been hit by a car at 70mph, and how it was a bit strange, because it was at 2.15p.m., on the wrong side of the Park, and she should have been back at work at 2 o'clock. They seemed surprised I hadn't heard, until I reminded them that I had been on holiday for two weeks. They will be even more surprised if they ever learn that it was I who paid for the commemorative tablet in the Gardens of Remembrance where her ashes are scattered. I go there most Friday evenings to sit with Stella.

© 2004 Val Wilson

MY NEW ROMANCE

Have you never felt fed up with your husband? Even if by normal standards he's a good husband? If you've been married for quite a while, haven't you wanted to try someone new? Or at least to find out if some-one else might find you still attractive? Let me tell you how, despite such thoughts, I failed to be even the tiniest bit un-faithful.

I've never stopped loving Gary, really I haven't, and even after six years I still enjoyed being married to him, but it had begun to seem just a bit unexciting. He was a good husband in so many ways – remembered to say he loved me every day, always noticed what I was wearing and told me how nice I looked, helped with the kids, took us on outings and holidays, and only left me alone in the evening once a fortnight when he went to a model aircraft club meeting. We never had to worry about money: he had a nice regular job as a computer salesman and he was very good at it. About once a year he would get a really good order and they would give him a bonus, and then we could buy something extra – a holiday, a spin dryer, or a kingsize bed.

I had nothing at all to complain about, nothing that I could really put my finger on, but something seemed to be missing. Where was the romance? It was all so regular and predictable. Every day I cooked the meals and tidied the house, played with the kids, washed the clothes and did the shopping. He went to work and brought home the money, and at weekends we spent time with the kids and maybe went on an outing somewhere. When you first meet some-one, you wonder if he likes you, and if you will see him tomorrow. And if you do, you're up in the clouds, but if he doesn't speak to you you're right down in the dumps. Then one day he asks you out, and you wonder if you will fall in love, or if you will meet some-one else even more wonderful. It's like a see-saw, up and down, excitement and depression, you never know what's going to happen next. Now I never had to worry if Gary loved me, or if I would see him again. He came home promptly at quarter to six every day.

The trouble really started, I think, when both the kids went to school. Abi was going to primary school now, and James had just started at nursery. I couldn't find a part-time job to fit in with their hours, and I didn't really have enough to do at home. On the day I am going to tell you about, it was about midday. The house was reasonably tidy, I had done all the shopping, and had an early lunch. There were plenty of things I could have done: looked underneath the rugs to see how much dust had accumulated there, cleaned the silver plated cutlery set which we never used, made those new cushion covers I'd planned for the lounge... things like that. But none of them seemed very urgent, and I just couldn't get down to it. The sun was shining outside and everything was warm – the air, the bricks of the house, our cat's fur. There was a playful breeze stirring the trees and twitching the curtains which made me feel restless. I drifted into the bedroom and looked at myself in the mirror, re-arranging my hair in various different ways. Then I decided to try on the new summer dress which I had bought last week but not worn yet. I studied my image in the glass. Yes, I had chosen well. The dress still convinced me I was pretty. The birds were singing in the garden, and I felt a sudden urge to spread my wings. I didn't want to go for a walk near home, where I went every day to the shops. There was a tube station just at the end of the road. Off I went, and bought a ticket to Regents Park.

A quarter of an hour later I was there, strolling among the brightly coloured flowers towards the lake, which shimmered cool and inviting in the sunlight. What a lot of people there were. Mothers played with young children, couples lay gazing into each other's eyes, senior citizens conscientiously walked their dogs. I settled down comfortably on a bench, and absorbed the warmth, the movement, the life of the ever-changing scene around me. Walking down the path towards me was a particularly handsome young man. My heart leapt. He caught my eye, and smiled. I smiled back.

'Hello there' he greeted me, 'That is a very pretty dress. Just the thing for the most beautiful girl in the Park'.

I blushed, and answered lightly 'I bet you say that to all the girls'.

'I certainly don't' he assured me 'Most of them would tell me exactly where to go if I did that but you I feel are simply waiting to be swept off your feet, carried off to a palace of white marble to be served with a cooling drink in a long slender glass'.

I laughed, feeling a surge of excitement. 'Where is this marble palace, then?' I asked 'and are you sure you have time?'

To be with you in your pretty dress? I'll make time, I'll steal time. Come on, it's this way'.

I followed obediently, unresisting. He led me across the grass to an extremely impressive building. We went in and crossed the foyer, which was indeed floored with white marble, to the bar area.

'Isn't it too expensive' I whispered anxiously.

'Nothing' he replied 'is too expensive for an occasion like this! A chance meeting on a perfect summer's day. It was obviously meant to be'.

He ordered me my favourite apple and mango juice without needing to ask, and it did indeed come in a long glass, with plenty of ice. The chilled liquid gliding down my throat was a welcome relief rom the heat of the sun outside. He ordered an Evian water for himself, just as I expected.

'Do you often come for a stroll in the Park at lunchtime?' he asked 'I've never seen you here before.'

'No'. I said 'This is the first time ever I've been here on a weekday without the children. Is this where you usually have your lunch?' I gazed into his gorgeous blue eyes as I questioned him, dreaming already of regular rendezvous in the white marble palace.

He laughed. 'I drink here occasionally with clients. Lunch is usually sandwiches outside in the Park, if I'm in the area, which I am, more often than not We should do this again, if you feel like stretching your kid-free wings a little'

My left hand rested on top of the bar, my wedding ring clearly visible on the third finger He covered it with his big strong man's hand, on which a wedding ring was also prominently displayed, and gave a little squeeze.

A thrill ran through me. 'I'd love that' I said.

'Perhaps we could make it a bit earlier next time?' he suggested. 'Must go now, if I'm to be home at the usual time. Got a few things to finish off at the office. Hadn't you better be moving too? Don't want to be late to pick up James, do you?'

I smiled at my husband, my new romance who still knew how to treat a lady. 'No', I said 'Of course not'.

© 2004 Val Wilson

PAUL WINSTANLEY

Originally from Somerset, Paul Winstanley spent most of his working life in government service, rounding off his career on secondment to the European Commission in Brussels. Married with two grown-up daughters, he is making the most of his retirement in Norfolk, a county he has always loved. A keen member of Dereham Operatic Society, he also enjoys family history research, photography and natural history as well as writing (and admiring his wife's water-colours!)

ON THE FACE OF IT

I am beginning to thoroughly mistrust my voice and face. In fact, I am wondering if I lost my face somewhere and picked up someone else's by mistake. You know, the way you do with briefcases and umbrellas. Of course, I still look like me, but the facial expressions I now seem to adopt bear no relation to how I feel.

For example, "Don't look so cross!" seems to issue from my wife's mouth more and more often these days, when I am not cross at all. A trifle miffed, maybe, over some triviality, or maybe just thoughtful, but not cross. I like to think I am of a rather equable, even tempered demeanour. But one sure way of making me cross is to accuse me of being cross. It's a bit like being told to stop shouting when I'm not, inevitably provoking me to bellow "*I am NOT shouting!*" And then feeling rather foolish, and then feeling resentment at being made to feel foolish, and then getting cross.

Similarly, I take pleasure in minor achievements. I recently installed an electric shower in my daughter's bathroom, for instance, and came home looking, I would have assumed, just slightly pleased with myself. I was soon disillusioned. "Oh for goodness sake look at him! Like the cat that got the cream! I suppose they cooed at you like turtle-doves!" No doubt I was smirking sickeningly, like a man feeling insufferably superior. But I wasn't.

On another occasion recently we had a visit from a very old friend (i.e. 'old' as in 'longstanding' not 'aged') and of course she had to bring her husband. Now George is a very worthy guy. He is really. I have to tell myself that. But his sole topics of conversation are cricket and World War II. And I know virtually nothing about cricket or World War II. I do my best. I really do. I try to make my eyes sparkle, and fix a look of polite interest on my face, but I'm afraid if a man goes on holiday to Australia, land of some of the most stupendous natural beauty in the world, and brings back only a collection of photographs of the war memorials and cricket pitches of the towns of southern Queensland, my enthusiasm for the conversation becomes somewhat limited. (What on earth attracts sparkling lively-minded women to marry such creatures?) So when they had gone I got it in the neck, of course. "You were very rude to George. You looked so cross and bored. I don't think you were listening to him half the time. I think he might have been upset." Oh, gee! How shall I ever live with myself!

Mind you, in the past I got away with it. My own face used to know my limited repertoire of mood swings. It could switch from mildly annoyed to mildly pleased to mildly sad to mildly interested. The whole gamut of the middle-class Englishman's emotions, in fact. I didn't cause offence to anybody. But not any more, it seems. This face I have now must have once belonged to an actor of the old 'expressionist' school. I recall as a keen member of an amateur drama group attending an evening course given by one such. He tried to teach us how to display Joy and Despair and Wonder and so on, but his strange facial contortions seemed to me to alternate only between looking completely bonkers and like a man who has just swallowed some unpleasant medicine. I was not an apt pupil. We had to do a test piece. 'The woodenness of Mr Winstanley's performance was complemented only by his dubious knowledge of the lines.' After that I usually got policeman parts.

Of course, if I am right, and I really have picked up the wrong face, there may be some poor fellow out there who has got my old face, and who, being possessed of the most towering emotions, leaping from the stygian depths of despair to to ethereal heights of ecstasy, is completely frustrated by being able to register only pleasure or mild dislike.

The problem is that it is by our faces and voices that people know us. When we meet someone for the first time, it is said, we form an opinion based solely on appearance, and something of this opinion will always remain, no matter how much we subsequently learn about that person's inner characteristics. That fatal configuration of hair, eyes, nose and mouth which makes up the physiognomy, and the noise that comes out of the mouth, creates that first immovable impression, and it is that whereby we are known and judged.

So goodness knows what impressions I am now giving off. If I feel just a bit happy I look sickeningly smug. If I am a bit shy and uncertain I look shifty and devious. If I am slightly irritated I scowl ferociously. So my face twists and writhes like a participant in a gurning contest. A Spitting Image puppet with a bull horn could not produce a worse caricature of the real me.

Maybe it's just as well I am living in a rural area again. When I came first to suburbia I noticed how 'switched off' people's faces were, a hard impassive mask. They had to be. You simply could not relate to thousands of people. But in a village you always nod and smile even to strangers, because there are so few. Perhaps my innate rusticity is reasserting itself. Goodbye bricks. Hello sticks. Joy and Wonder. Calm and Contentment. For a while anyway.

© 2004 Paul Winstanley

CANDLE IN THE DARK

The tenebrous interior of the cathedral rendered Roger temporarily blind as he walked through the doorway out of the blazing Spanish sun. He stood in an alcove formed by the stone portal against the wall, out of the way of the milling tourists, and as his eyes accustomed to the gloom he yawned and looked unenthusiastically at the numerous statues of saints, the carvings, the massive stone columns, and the medieval paintings depicting biblical characters glowering down from the walls.

It wasn't really his idea of a holiday, traipsing round churches and palaces and art galleries and museums, but Ruth loved all that stuff, and on this holiday whatever Ruth wanted Ruth was going to get. At least here there was a welcome atmosphere of peace, insofar as that was possible in a tourist-trap like this at the height of the summer season.

Roger looked craningly round for his wife among all the camera-clicking sight-seers, their continuous blue flashes stabbing pitiless holes in the orisonous softness. She had gone ahead while he had cashed in some travellers cheques and bought cigarettes. But she didn't seem to be here. Strange. Her white shirt and ash-blonde hair should be easy to spot. Surely she wouldn't have wandered off somewhere else. This was where they'd arranged to meet. Perhaps she'd gone to the gift shop or somewhere. Typical Ruth. Always buying presents and postcards and souvenirs.

He sat heavily on a pew. Anyway she seems to be enjoying herself, he thought. It was going quite well, really. But even as he said these words to himself a nasty little voice inside him said 'Who are you kidding?' No, it wasn't really going well. It wasn't really going anywhere. Ruth and he weren't close. During the day they were no more than affable, pleasant, like two singleton tourists who might have been thrown together on a package holiday.

It was five weeks since that dreadful morning when Ruth had woken him up and confessed to her affair with some guy from the golf club. He remembered her agonised face, her tearful voice blurting it all out, and crying at him to hit her. As if he could. He'd rather chop his hand off.

The affair was now ended, but they were not reconciled. Roger knew his wife's heart still yearned elsewhere, and he had hit on the idea of this holiday, as part of the process of mending their marriage. A break, away from everything, doing all the things that she liked, and then back to make a fresh start. He had booked it in secret, and presented it to her, tickets, hotel reservations, brochures, the whole caboodle, as a grand surprise one morning. He had looked desperately at her face as he had spread out the papers. Was there a spark of real joy there? Would this begin to reawaken her love? Of course she had smiled and thanked him, and given him a dutiful kiss. But Roger's heart had sunk.

His reverie was now broken as he noticed a woman who had been kneeling at the altar rail. She got up and removed some sort of black cloth or scarf from her head and shoulders. As she turned he saw her profile and her hair caught the light from the nearby ranks of votive candles. It was Ruth. What on earth was she doing? She went over to the candles, folding the cloth. She exchanged smiles with an elderly black-clad woman who was sitting beside them and gave the cloth to her. The old woman gave her a candle and she lit it from one of the others already in the iron rack, and placed it in a vacant holder. She paused, watching the flame as it struggled precariously with the eddying air currents until it settled. Then she turned to walk down an aisle away from the altar.

Roger stood up and her eyes widened as she saw him. A startled guilt-stricken look crossed her face before she quickly masked it with a smile.

"You weren't long. I thought you'd be ages."

"There wasn't a queue at the bank for once." said Roger. He nodded enquiringly at the altar. "What was all that, then? And what was that veil thing?"

"It's a mantilla. You wear it to pray."

They walked out into the sun. The noise of traffic and people assaulted the ears like a hi-fi suddenly switched on at full blast in a quiet room.

"The fine art museum's up here." she said, turning into a narrow alley. The noise subsided to a muffled roar.

Roger could not stop himself asking the question. though a premonition told him he should not.

"And did you?"

"Did I what?"

"Pray."

There was a pause. Then a barely audible "Yes."

The voice spoke in Roger's mind. The voice that was always right, warning him when he was heading for trouble. "Leave it! Leave it!" it said.

But he couldn't leave it.

"For us?"

She didn't answer, and Roger knew why. One of Ruth's failings, or endearing characteristics, depending how you looked at it, was that she found it impossible to tell white lies. She was not the slightest bit deceitful, and Roger had loved her for it once.

"For him, then."

Ruth turned to look at him, and nodded, emotion flooding her face.

"Satisfied?" said the mocking voice.

But Roger wasn't satisfied. He had to know.

"Why?" His voice was hard and challenging.

She stopped walking and turned to face him. "To help me to say goodbye."

She walked on, a pace in front of him, so that she did not see the tear roll down Roger's cheek. He wiped it roughly away with the back of his hand. Control! Control, man! Get a grip!

Roger bought a glossy guidebook for Ruth and two entrance tickets at the fine art museum, and trailed miserably behind her as she slowly went from painting to painting. Then came the sculpture galleries. Roger's feet ached and he felt like slumping onto one of those benches and going to sleep. I'm just not a culture vulture, he thought. Give me sun, sea and sangria any day. But he said nothing. This was for Ruth. He wondered if Thing had been a culture freak. He didn't know his name. Didn't want to. But he bet he was. All arty-farty and cultured.

His mind went back to the cathedral. Neither he nor Ruth were religious, though she had been educated at a catholic convent school. That's where she had got all that candle stuff from. But he found himself moved at the memory of her at that altar rail. It was so Ruth, somehow. And he felt his eyes moisten as he realised how much he loved her, and would always love her. But God, how to win back her heart? Not just a reconciliation, but really win her.

After two and a half leaden hours even Ruth had had enough fine art and he walked with some relief back to the hotel with her. The midday meal was just salady nibbly stuff. Typical continental. Oh, for some bangers and mash. Afterwards, Ruth was booked for a hair-do and a 'facial' whatever that was.

"I'll go and buy an English paper." said Roger.

Ten minutes later he stood looking down at the mocking candle flames at the cathedral altar. He tried to see which was the one she had lit but gave up. The woman in black looked at him expressionlessly.

"Now just what do you think you're going to do?" said the voice. " Ask the Angel Gabriel to bump off Lover-Boy with a thunderbolt?"

"Shut up!" thought Roger, so fiercely that he articulated involuntarily. A pair of camera-festooned Japanese looked round with startled almond eyes.

Just what the hell did you do here? Was there a special prayer or something? He couldn't see any prayers written on the wall. Anyway they'd be in Spanish wouldn't they. His mouth twisted into the wryest of smiles.

He offered a handful of coins to the woman in black. She selected two and gave him a candle.

Roger wedged it in a holder and made sure the flame had caught. He stepped back. Ruth had knelt at the rail, but he couldn't bring himself to do that.

"You gormless prat!" said the merciless voice.

Roger tried to remember the Lords Prayer from school assembly days. He gabbled off some of the phrases to himself, desperately shutting out the voice. That would have to do. He didn't know any more.

He sat in the front pew to regain his composure before leaving. He ought to make up a prayer of his own. He shut his eyes.

"Please – Please just let her – just – make her love me – "

But the words wouldn't come. And the voice was getting louder, piercing his brain. "You prat! You prat! You pathetic prat!" He could stand it no more, got up and rushed out into the welcoming secular sunshine and din.

Ruth saw him from their hotel balcony, coming from the direction of the cathedral. She knew he would go back there. Knew what he had done. If only he hadn't seen her at the altar. She knew he'd never understand. And it was only a little gesture, for goodness sake. Just to help her say goodbye to the man who had brought her such joy. Joy she knew she would never have again. Why did he have to go and destroy it? She wondered if he'd got the right candle. Had he just blown it out, she wondered. Or had he pulled it out and ground it under foot. Not that it mattered. He would never tell her, and she would never ask.

She looked at his slumped shoulders as he walked lifelessly up the street, then turned, fought down her tears, and moved resignedly back into the room.

© 2004 Paul Winstanley

FOOD FOR THOUGHT

I am beginning to hate dinner parties. The trouble with dinner parties is the dinner. Food and cooking, instead of being just an unsung necessity of life, in recent years has become a popular hobby, and is now an obsession, the subject of a huge output of television programs, books and health advice which has even spawned new food-related psychological disorders.

All this has had a peculiar effect upon people, women in particular. On the one hand, women no longer spend most of their lives in the kitchen, yet on another, more insidious level, their lives seem to be more dominated by food than ever their mothers' were. Everything has to be done so professionally now, and in accordance with mores which until recently never existed. Fat, carbohydrates and sugars are monitored to the point of neurosis. Cheerful carnivores are subjected to the strictures of sanctimonious vegetarians. 'E is for Additives', or rather, E is for Excessive Concern about Additives.

And the effect upon dinner parties is catastrophic. When I go to a private dinner-party with friends the primary purpose for me is not the food. Of course I expect there to be food, because if there isn't I shall get hungry, and won't enjoy the wine. But it doesn't have to be cordon bleu, just hot and tasty. The real purpose of the party, the reason I am bothering to venture out on a wet winter night, is not the food. It is the company. It is the gossip, the discussion, the jokes, the news, the bonhomie. Or it should be. Yet so many women behave, both as hostesses and guests, as if they think that the pudding club is not just something they join when pregnant. It is in fact the food which ruins the party, and that is not because everyone has dire need of Alka-Seltzer. The very opposite in fact.

It is usually a female guest who starts the rot. The conversation is ping-ponging happily about. Holiday plans. Hobbies. Someone's new house. Someone's new baby. Then it comes. A woman smacks her lips appreciatively. "This is nice, Lorraine." she says. "What did you use? Dripping or vegetable oil? And what's that delicious spicey taste?" Lorraine then simpers and explains in detail how she spent three and a half hours making the sauce, including how she improved on what Delia Smith said on TV. Karen then chimes in to explain how she always double sifts the flour and why she only ever uses Greek extra virgin olive oil. That is a signal for Hayley to explain a method of making roux which her mother told her and which has been passed down the female line in her family for at least five generations. And so it goes on. The subject of the dinner party conversation is the dinner itself. Non-cooks relapse into silence and moodily feeding their faces. So they eat too much, partly as a compensation for feeling rather bored and partly with the vague idea that it is expected of them, given that so much talk and effort has been invested in the food. Thus the after dinner conversation does not flow and sparkle as half the guests are just trying to fight off the dreaded doze reaction. People leave early, and the general consensus of home-going couples is that it was all a bit dull, and anyway it was obviously tinned tomatoes and everyone knows you don't use oil with aubergines. And we never did ask about Matthew's trip to Turkestan or Fiona's new job.

But, ladies, if you are really determined to ruin your dinner party, what may be termed the Martyred Cook Gambit never fails. Picture the scene. You have served a perfectly cooked meal bang on time. The wine is chambré, the plates are hot. Your guests like each other, and ooze pleasurable anticipation. You wait until everyone is served and munching contentedly, and then you ask in detail if everything is alright. Does the gravy taste alright? Is the meat alright? Are the rolls alright? Are the vegetables alright? And so on. There will be a chorus of "Wonderful!" and "Delicious!" with contented mumbles and nodding heads. You then say "Only of course I can't tell because I cooked it, you see. I can't enjoy anything I have prepared myself. It completely spoils it for me, you know. Cooking it takes *all* the pleasure out of it. I never enjoy eating it. But, there, as long as you are all enjoying it, that's all that matters of course." You then toy listlessly with the food on your own plate, while exhorting everyone else to eat gargantuan helpings, in view of all the effort and pain that has been expended upon the preparation. Everyone will of course start praising your food to the skies. The very gods themselves were never served so well. It was worth all your labour and pain. You, of course, must remain unmollified. You can occasionally smile graciously and say "Well, of course, I'm just glad you like it." or "Well, as long as it was really all worth while." And if the guests really do look as if they are in danger of being reassured, and the praise starts faltering, you can stoke things up again by saying something like "Of course it may just be me, but I think it's a bit too salty." A full-blooded debate on saltiness will then ensue, with the cooks each expounding their personal philosophy on optimum salinity levels, while the non-cooks sigh and wish to goodness that you had just sent out for some pizza.

I find all this particularly frustrating because I have never been a 'foodie.' I was brought up by an old-fashioned "eat-what's-put-in-front-of-you-and-none-of-your-nonsense" type of mother, so I developed very few fads and fancies. Grub was grub and all I asked was an adequate supply. It is an attitude I have taken with me into adult life. Food is simply fuel, no more.

So lighten up, ladies! We non-foodie non-cooks want to talk to you. We want to know if you've seen the latest Woody Allen film, whether you ever read Proust, and did you get the new P.R. job you were after, and what are your views on the Euro, and did that woman across the road really run off with the president of her husband's golf club? And we hope you might actually be interested in *us*! In talking to us about something other than second helpings and whether that's enough potatoes. Why else have you invited us to your home? Did you just think we looked ill-nourished?

But there is hope. I know of one star shining in the blackness, in the form of a lady of my acquaintance who has reinvented herself. She is undoubtedly a superb cook. She never used to serve less than two or three varieties of home-made sauce or salad dressing, or freshly made biscuits, or sausage roll, or what-have-you. All this was fine, of course, but limiting. She really thought that all she had to offer her friends were her culinary skills.

But now she happily serves shop pre-prepared. And cheerfully admits to it. Sometimes she even sends out for a take-away. And very good they are too. The conversation now turns, not on to how to make taramasalata, but to the Meaning of Life and Love and Everything. She has taken up creative writing, and has just finished a novel. She is learning music. Whether all this is a direct result of her new attitude to food I don't know, but it certainly enriches her conversation. She seems to be such an interesting person. Far tastier than her cooking, in fact.

There is nothing new about all this. Charles Dickens knew it. Remember the dinner party scene in David Copperfield? Where poor scatty 'child-wife' Dora serves unopened oysters and near-raw mutton which no-one could eat? And did her dear 'Dodie' love her any the less for it? If anything it made him even more besotted.

Pass the monosodium glutamate, please!

A response, by Gina Gutteridge

As those who were here last time may recall, one writer's witty piece on dinner parties produced something of an attack of indigestion at this particular place setting. As I latter mulled over this case of heartburn, I was somewhat curious as to its cause. As the writer said guardedly to me later: "It certainly seemed to touch a spot!". Indeed.

Paul's piece centred on dinner parties being ruined by chattering women, obsessed with how mine hostess had cooked such a splendid repast – with no area of culinary expertise too trivial for consideration and discussion, thus ruining all chance of an evening's more erudite, intellectual and intelligent conversation.

My equally erudite comments of "I personally couldn't give a toss what happens in the kitchen" and "Chris now does a lot of the cooking" and "Were none of these dinner parties ever cooked by men?" does gloss over the fact that for the first 20 years or so of our marriage, I was the 'angel in the kitchen' and did everything therein. This was apart from the odd birthday meal when the other half could really excel himself with a steak dinner, if we didn't happen to go out to celebrate.

Then, about 10 years ago, due to a combination of different personal factors affecting both of us, Chris took over the reins of

Gutteridge cuisine (supposedly partly as therapy) and I worked and studied. So now that we have two daughters over twenty, equally if not more capable in the kitchen than either of us, whoever is at home at the time and feels like cooking on a particular night will do so. A general rule that has emerged from this is that whoever is cooking, has the right to cook something they like – and the rest of the family are just grateful that somebody else has braved the rigours of fridges, freezer, cooker, vegetable rack and a really mean electric tin opener, whose only aim in life is to amputate any dallying fingers!

So, what is the spot that the thought of all these elegant soirees touched? I could imagine from Paul's wonderful description – these domestic goddesses, a la Delia and Nigella (but darling, it's so easy – anybody could do it!) sitting around beautifully polished tables, silverware and cut glass sparkling in the soft candlelight; the ladies beautifully clothed and coiffured – in raptures over sauces (oh! roux the day!); steamed scallops and saffroned squid. Oh bliss! Oh rapture! Pass the Alka Seltzer, please. But, where are the Lloyds, the Ainsleys and the Garys in this equation? Does he never go to a dinner party where the husband or male partner does the honours?

And what about our dinner parties? Well, from the time we were first married, we have always had friends around for meals and over the years, and there have been some memorable occasions, some of which have warranted the title 'dinner party'. But, oh boy! The work, the stress, the attention to detail to get everything just right. So that gradually, these grand evenings of soft music and candlelight have been replaced by a more casual and laid-back approach. That isn't to say that we are not greatly appreciative when we are the recipients, but we're sorry, we just don't go there ourselves, anymore.

Part of the answer to my own personal puzzle, strangely enough, came the other week from a girl working in a pub where we were having a delicious celebratory birthday lunch. She was having a conversation across the bar with a group of friends about shopping and she solemnly said: "I don't think I'm a proper woman because I don't like clothes shopping". And perhaps this is it, the well marinated spot, that I feel a failed female because of lack of interest in culinary capers. No matter that I possibly have more interesting attributes, the guilt simmers away.

Younger daughter sprang to my aid along these same lines only recently, when we were visiting my father-in-law. He had been extolling the virtues of one of my two sisters-in-law, both of whom are extremely domesticated with five- star cookability skills. One of them had been telling him how she had been showing one of her four grand-daughters how to make Christmas puddings. In fact, these puddings from this particular sister-in-law have been revered in the family, somewhat like the Holy Grail, throughout my married life, but not being especially mad about Christmas pud, I've never been very bothered and happily buy one every year. On this occasion, I muttered under my breath something along the lines of – 'I've never made a Christmas pudding in my life, thank God' and younger daughter, with a flashing smile, quickly added: 'I'm sure you've had better things to do with your time, Mum, haven't you?" All misdemeanours committed by said off-spring for the past five years were immediately forgiven.

Mind you, I'm on dangerous ground – my grandmother was a Paris-trained, Cordon-Bleu cook, who worked at Sandringham and Buck House, and is probably turning in her grave if she is hearing this. But, each to his own. I've been told by an afficianado of such things that I make 'a real mean vegetable soup'; and daughters extol the virtues of my quiche and roast chicken. Perhaps interviewing Lord Melchett, Sir Malcolm Arnold and Bradbury, Louis de Berniere, Hinge and Bracket, Gary Wilmot, The Beverley Sisters, Roy Hattersley, Tony Soper, the Pope – (no, only joking!) Stephen Fry, Germaine Greer and other miscellaneous celebrities have made for more interesting after-eight chat than, darling, do tell, what flavour-base did you use for this trifle? (Gracious – and you thought you had to go to a dinner party to name drop!). By the way, did you know, Mr. Fry is passionate about commercial kitchen equipment and could keep any dinner party in pommes frites with tales of his commercial potato-peeling machine? Pass the mints, please!

© 2004 Paul Winstanley

ELVERFORD
Read at bedtime at your peril!

"Can you take me out to Elverford tomorrow, dear, please?" My elderly Aunt Enid looked at me, hopefully but uncertainly, as she spoke these words. I knew why she was so diffident, but I could never have imagined what such an innocent request presaged. A few short weeks would see our family touched by an evil which nearly destroyed us and left me permanently scarred in both mind and body. I do not think that up until then I had really believed in evil. I do now.

Elverford had once been the family home. It was remote and beautiful, truly an enchanted spot. I had never lived there, but my father and aunts had as children, and I had cycled there sometimes when I was a schoolboy. The stone and thatch farm-house was perched at the top of a small steeply sloping valley. There was an orchard next to it with trees of some long-forgotten strain which produced the tastiest fruit I had ever known, and nearby was a brown stream where moorhens bred and herons fished. Myriads of butterflies and dragonflies complemented the abundant wild flowers in the adjoining field.

My father and his two sisters had spent their childhood here. Neither of the girls had married and they had lived all their lives together. The nicknames bestowed upon them by my father were very apposite. Aunt Chloë was Miss Grave-and-Grim and Aunt Enid was Miss Sweet-and-Sensible. Aunt Enid was my favourite aunt, but I was always afraid of Aunt Chloë, who had died just one month ago, rather suddenly. Since I was now Aunt Enid's only close relative, it was natural she should ask me a small favour, but she would never have dared ask to be taken to Elverford if Chloë were still alive.

Chloë had loved Elverford with a consuming intensity, and regarded the present owners, although they were related to family, as usurpers. Their name was Skinner, I recalled. Something of Chloë's attitude toward them was shared by the rest of our family, so that though I barely remembered them they had been so demonised in my mind by relatives that even now I could hardly think of them without animosity.

It was a fine late summer afternoon when we drew up outside Elverford. A thin anxious-looking woman with wispy grey hair waited at the door as we climbed out of the car and walked up the path. I just recognised Nora Skinner from years back. Time had not been kind to her. Having shaken hands formally under my aunt's expectant gaze, we were shown into a large sitting room. I noticed immediately a hospital-like smell of urine and disinfectant before hearing the unmistakable noise of a piece of crockery breaking on the floor behind me.

I turned to see a dishevelled and distressed-looking man half-lying, half-sitting in a wooden armchair. A board had been screwed across the arms of the chair to form a tray, against which the man's hand was scraping and knocking. He was trying to raise himself to a full sitting position but the unco-ordinated flailing of his arm only succeeded in knocking off a plate to join a broken cup. He became more and more agitated, groaning and dribbling from the corner of his mouth, the light wooden armchair jerking and creaking as he tried to move his body.

With a cry of "Oh, George, do try to be careful!" Nora rushed over to him. Aunt Enid joined her but George Skinner would not be calmed, to the obvious puzzlement of the two women. "Whatever's the matter with you, George?" said Nora, then to my aunt "I don't think this was a good idea, Aunt Enid." 'This' was, of course, my presence there, but George Skinner didn't seem to be concerned about me. His face was turned toward the window. "Oh No! Not again! He's gone and dirtied himself again!" cried Nora. The note of hysteria was unmistakeable. This was obviously a frequent occurrence.

"Then we'll just have to clean him up," said Aunt Enid, ever practical, ever helpful. She looked at me imploringly, but I felt no obligation to these people.

"Perhaps I should go outside for a bit," I said lamely, and walked back out of the still open front door.

I stood by the car, lit a cigarette and looked at the house. Dusk was falling, and the huge sycamore tree by the sitting room window was blowing in the evening breeze. My gaze was caught by something odd about the waving branches near the window. I squinted skywards. What was it?

Then my knees felt weak and I nearly fainted. Clearly visible in the top pane of the window, somehow part of but separate from the reflection of the tossing leaves, was the face of Aunt Chloë. She was looking into the room, straight down at George Skinner. I could still hear his agitated cries, and the voices of the two women vainly trying to understand what was the matter with him. Then the face turned and looked directly at me, and I broke into a cold sweat. Never had I seen such a look of malign triumph, of pure undiluted gloating on any face before. She was delighting, glorying in Skinner's plight as if she were somehow responsible for it. Her eyes shone, and her lips were parted in a twisted grin. As I watched, the face seemed to grow and distort, becoming more and more hideous, the face of a fiend permeating the whole tree. Then it was gone, and Aunt Enid was standing in front of me, telling me I was a fat lot of good in a crisis.

I felt very sick, and allowed her to lead me, child-like, back into the house. Skinner was quiet. "He's had one of his pills," said Nora. Her offer of tea and sandwiches was made without enthusiasm, and my excuse about having to get back to keep an appointment was accepted without even formal protest. I would have vomited at the sight of food. Both women looked at me coldly. No doubt I looked weak and useless. I confirmed all their country women's prejudices. I was a typical squeamish male, hopeless when it came to the realities of birth, sickness and death with which it was women's lot to cope.

Aunt Enid apologised to Nora, promised to visit again when she could (another glare for me) and we set off wordlessly for home.

"How long has he been like that?" I asked, after a few miles.

"Only a few weeks."

"Very sudden then." I said.

"He was as right as rain a month ago." came the reply. "A severe stroke, they reckon." Aunt Enid paused, then said quietly " 'Twas the week Chloë died." Neither of us said a further word all the way home, but my mind was awhirl. Old half-forgotten memories came flooding back.

Aunt Chloë had been a deeply unhappy and disturbed woman. Her family nickname described her well. I had never seen her laugh. It is true she had known tragedy when she was young. Her fiancé had been found drowned in a local lake in circumstances never clearly resolved, and there is no doubt that this had affected her permanently, but the thing which really gnawed at her soul was the loss of Elverford.

My grandfather's first wife, the mother of my father and the aunts, had died young, and my grandfather then married a widow with one daughter, Nora. When Nora married George Skinner, they had moved into Elverford with my grandfather and Nora's mother, my grandfather's second wife. This irked Aunt Chloë enough, but when my grandfather sold Elverford to Skinner she never got over it. The sale was in return for an understanding whereby the Skinners guaranteed him a home at Elverford and would look after him in his old age. The arrangement had worked well enough, but Aunt Chloë thought she had been cheated out of her inheritance, despite the generosity of my grandfather, who had made sufficient provision to give the unmarried sisters a secure home.

As she grew older, Aunt Chloë had become obsessed with Elverford, until she was barely sane. She withdrew more and more into her own little world of bitterness and resentment, ranting endlessly about her childhood home. And dear patient Aunt Enid would wearily point out that Elverford was their father's to dispose of as he wished, that it had been sold quite legally, and there was an end to it. Were it not for Enid's fortitude and care, her sister would certainly have been institutionalised.

George Skinner died a few weeks after our ill-fated visit. I went to the funeral, because it would have looked rather pointed to certain cousins not to, and then Aunt Enid asked me to go back with her to the wake at Elverford.

Nora had decided to sell Elverford in order to buy a small flat near her daughter. With what some of the relatives made clear they thought was indecent haste, the sale literature had already been commissioned and Nora was simply waiting for the solicitors' permission to put the auction arrangements in hand. She even passed round a few black-and-white photocopies of the agents' photographs of the house. I wanted to get away quickly and went to take my leave of Nora, who was talking to Aunt Enid. "I'm staying on a few days to help Nora" she said.

Nora looked at the photograph still in my hand and said "Do you like it? Keep it if you like. Be nice if you bought the place, wouldn't it?"

"Fat chance." I said. The three of us stood looking at the photograph. It showed the front of the house, the fence, and the sycamore tree to the left of the front door.

"Chloë planted that tree." said Aunt Enid quietly.

"Did she?" I said. "I never knew that."

"Oh, yes. When she was small. Thought the world of it, she did. Wouldn't let Dad prune it, or anything." I looked at the tree in the photograph, and then the nausea I had felt a few weeks earlier came on so suddenly it made me gasp. In the photocopy, the leafy outer branches of the tree mingled indistinctly with the tiles on the roof of the house behind it. I could see Aunt Chloë's face there quite clearly, but it wasn't the same as last time. The face was higher up, and it wasn't grinning. It seemed to be looking to the left of the photograph.

"Were you there when this was taken?" I heard myself saying.

"We were sitting on the orchard stile with the grand-children, watching." said Nora. "Why? What on earth are you staring at?" They both looked perplexedly at me and at the photograph. I could say nothing, and had to sit heavily on a nearby chair.

Aunt Enid saw me anxiously into my car. I assured her I would be all right. She wasn't convinced, but had to hurry away to help Nora with more sandwiches for the guests after telling me I was looking "peaky" lately, and that I should see the doctor to get a "bottle of tonic." Dear Aunt Enid! I drove off slowly down the lane, noting the position of the orchard stile, which would certainly have been off-camera to the left of the photograph. I dared not look at the sycamore.

I stopped at a lay-by on the way home, and without looking at it again threw the crumpled photograph into a waste bin. I just had to get a grip on myself or I should go mad. Nevertheless a feeling of unease which I had never known before in my life just would not leave me, and somehow I was not very surprised to get Aunt Enid's distressed telephone call a few days later.

Apparently Enid had gone with Nora's daughter and her family to Elverford to help pack and remove some furniture and other items. The two boys had gone off to play while the van was being loaded, and had been climbing trees. The elder of the two had fallen to the ground and hurt himself.

"Where was the tree they were climbing?" I said.

"In front of the house." came the reply. "The sycamore."

I broke into a sweat as I listened to my aunt's measured, matter-of-fact narrative. The boy was still unconscious, and she had gone with Nora and her daughter to the hospital, from where she was speaking. The three women were all going to stay by his bedside until he came to. The younger boy seemed to have been very badly shaken by the accident, even though he was apparently uninjured. Kept crying and saying he'd seen a monster, or something. The effect of too much television, in my aunt's opinion. The hospital had given them a sedative for him, and his father had taken him home to put him to bed. Aunt Enid wanted me to come to the hospital for the keys to Elverford and make sure everything was secured. They had left in such confusion she was worried the doors and windows weren't all shut. Typical Aunt Enid!

I put down the 'phone, and a strange sense of purpose enveloped me. The disabling feeling of unease dropped away. There was no doubt about what must be done, and it was I who must do it, and I must do it now. I went out to the garage and found the axe we used to split the logs before gas central heating. Useless. It would take all day, and anyway I was no steel-muscled lumberjack.

I discarded the axe and found the roof rack we used for camping holidays. Having secured it to the car, I found some binder twine and tied my longest ladder to it. I threw work-gloves and a can of petrol into the car and drove to a camping shop where I bought a length of orange nylon rope and a quartz halogen torch. The next stop was a tool and plant hire shop, where I took the largest petrol-driven chain-saw they had.

At the hospital, to my great relief, Aunt Enid had thoughtfully left the keys with the front reception desk. No need to talk to her, therefore, and risk losing my nerve. By this time dusk was falling, and a wind was freshening. Rain was obviously imminent, but at least that meant that no-one was likely to be able to see what I was going to do. By the time I turned into the lane for Elverford it was quite dark, and the wind had become a full gale, slamming the torrential rain almost horizontally against the car.

When the house came into view, I could just make out the sycamore branches heaving violently in the wind, occasionally knocking against the house wall. This was going to be awkward. The direction of the wind would make it impossible to fell the tree away from the house.

I decided to try lopping a few branches. This was foolish of course, in such conditions, but it seemed imperative somehow to at least start the job, before my resolve failed me. I carried the saw over to the tree. By the light of the torch I identified one branch which was almost low enough for me to reach from the ground, and I reasoned the tree itself was big enough to shelter me from the worst of the rain while I cut it. I put a metal bucket I found by the house wall upside down on the ground under the branch, and embedded the base of the torch in the ground so that it shone upwards on the place where the branch grew from the trunk. The wind seemed to be getting stronger, and the tree's branches were tossing and creaking wildly. In my heightened emotional state it seemed to me that the agitated boughs knew of the threat below them. I balanced awkwardly on the bucket. A sudden gust of wind lashed a swatch of stinging leafy twigs across my face. I fell rather than stepped off the bucket. What on earth was I doing? This was madness. And yet it seemed essential not to give in. The tree was willing me to fail, and I must defeat it now, or be lost. If I could just get this branch, this one branch.......

I remounted the bucket, pushed the saw's primer, and pulled the starter cord. It fired immediately. Its harsh buzz and impatient vibration in my hand somehow encouraged me, and bravado (or was it desperation) finally defeated caution. I raised the saw above my head toward the base of the branch, clearly visible in the torch light.

Just as the saw began to bite into the bark, the torch beam moved. I cursed as the torch began to keel over in the soft earth. The powerful beam arced away from the branch, and straight into my eyes, blinding me totally. And out of the light came the face. It erupted from the dazzling whiteness, this time picked out in hideous oil-slick colours, moving and changing like some nightmarish kaleidoscope. I screwed my eyes tightly shut, but it made no difference. Reds became blues, yellow became green. The eyes darkened from pale orange to scarlet to intense crimson, boring into my brain, hypnotising, paralysing me, willing me to fall. I felt myself teetering forward, my face thrown toward the racing toothed chain.

Desperately I pushed the saw away from my face, involuntarily squeezing the trigger. The saw roared and bucked violently backwards. Feeling myself overbalancing I instinctively threw the saw back over my shoulder before falling and rolling over in the muddy grass. The torch light disappeared, and I could see nothing in the driving rain and blackness.

My pathetic bravado had now evaporated. I was winded, wet through and shivering with fright or cold or both. My hands were numb. I abandoned the saw and torch, and staggered up to the front door of the house. With some difficulty I fumbled the keys from my pocket and let myself in.

Aunt Enid's fears were, of course, groundless. The door had been locked. I flicked on the light. No windows were open, but the house was unheated and in my wet clothes I felt chilled to the marrow. I went down the hall toward the back of the house and tried the kitchen door, which was also safely locked. Then I turned back, and cried out as I caught sight of myself in the hall mirror. The whole of one side of my head was covered in blood. It was running down my neck and a red stain was spreading onto my shirt and jacket. I went up to the mirror. The blood was coming from my ear, most of which seemed to have been torn right away, though I had not been conscious of any pain, just an all-pervading coldness. Then, despite the cold, I broke into a sweat, and felt the now familiar nausea as the face materialised from behind my own in the mirror. It writhed and grimaced as before, but then its mouth opened, and a black reptilian tongue reached for my lacerated ear. I heard myself scream and leapt back against the wall, looking desperately away from the mirror, but this time the face was everywhere. It mocked me from the pattern in the carpet. It was in the folds of the curtains. It bobbed and leered from a vase of chrysanthemums. It was in the plaster mouldings on the ceiling. It peered from a polished brass gong. There was no escaping it. The sound of the wind outside intensified and grew higher in pitch, as the mouths of all the faces twisted and gaped, shrieking at me through the wind. The sheer volume of sound paralysed me, engulfed me, till I thought my ears must burst.

I felt myself falling backwards, and felt a stab of pain in my head. My torn ear had caught on something. The hall-stand toppled onto me, blood dripping from one peg, and suddenly I could move. I struggled to my feet and stumbled back down the hall. The flimsy kitchen door gave easily to my shoulder (I was beyond fumbling with keys) and I fell into the blackness. I staggered forward till my legs collapsed, and knelt in the rain, shaking as if palsied.

From behind me, above the wind's howl, came a wrenching, tearing sound, then a sound like rocks falling, with splintering wood and breaking glass. I cried out as a ground-shaking crash followed. The house lights went out. There were several more heavy thumps and shattering noises, then just the howling wind.

I stayed crouched on the grass, till my helpless trembling subsided and I was able to get up and feel my way slowly back to the kitchen door, but there was no door, only a tangle of twigs and wet leaves. I groped my way along the wall, forced my way through some sort of shrubbery at the side of the house onto the lane, and walked down till I blundered into the car.

Once inside I switched on the headlights. I could see little, but it was clear that the whole middle section of the roof of the house had disappeared. The huge tree had virtually cut it in half. Where the front porch and doorway had been, a mass of soil and roots bulked against the wall. As I watched, the whole right hand gable collapsed onto the twisted branches. The wind seemed to have subsided slightly, and the demon howl was gone, but the rain continued unabated.

I was shivering uncontrollably again, and in no state to drive, so I locked all the doors, and sat moaning in my rain-soaked clothes, dabbing at my now throbbing ear with a sticky sodden handkerchief. I watched the rain run down the car windows against the blackness. Aunt Chloë's face had gone, and somehow I knew it would never return. No-one would ever live in Elverford again.

© 2004 Paul Winstanley

GROUNDLESS FORCE

"The kiss of the sun for pardon
The song of the birds for mirth
One is nearer God's heart in a garden
Than anywhere else on earth."

This repellent piece of doggerel can be bought, inscribed on lumps of concrete moulded to look like lumps of stone, at our local garden centre. Quite apart from the incompetence of the rhymester who produced it (for example, one can only assume s/he used the absurd word 'pardon' because it was the only rhyme for 'garden' s/he could come up with) the sentiment is so untrue. Gardeners who garden only when the sun kisses them will not have weed-free flower-beds. Not in the British climate anyway. You have to get out there in your mud-caked wellies in the drizzle and gloom to ensure you sow on time, and transplant on time, and yank those thistles out when the soil is moist.

We'll leave out the mirthful song of the birds for the moment. I shall only be accused of being pedantic if I point out that birdsong is mainly proclamation of territory and warning signals, and is thus a deadly serious business for the birds. Nothing mirthful about it. And certainly gardens are not bird-friendly places, as we shall see.

It's the God bit that really leaves me gasping. Because God doesn't like gardens. He really doesn't. I reckon he got disheartened after chucking Adam and Eve out of Eden. 'Put the gardening tools away, lads!' he said to the angels. 'Gardening's no fun any more and it's just wasted on these two. We'll go for Nature instead.' So now God likes jungles and swamps and wildernesses. You can tell that by the way he completely erases all trace of human tillage from any garden if given half the chance. Leave a garden alone and see what happens. The weeds and grass smother the artificial products of horticultural propagation. Lawns turn into pasture. Brambles and nettles reclaim the flowerbeds, turning them into no-go areas for any except the most determined humans. There is an old joke about a vicar who, seeing a parishioner working hard in his garden, sententiously remarks how nice it is to see God and man working together. "But you should have seen it when God had it all to himself!" comes the heartfelt reply.

Gardening is just a specialised form of control freakery. Consider for a moment what gardeners have to do. To make the garden in the first place they have to remove all the grass and trees and wild flowers. All the silly things God put there, in fact. And the tools of their trade are fearsome. Diggers, bulldozers, chainsaws and flamethrowers. Then having established the garden, much of their time is spent just killing things.

Take weeds, for example. Now a weed is a plant, that's all. A little innocent leafy green plant which thrusts its tender shoots trustingly up toward that kissing sun. But the gardener zaps it with chemicals such as aminotriazole, paraquat, or dichlobenil. Some of these, like dioxin, are carcinogenic. Now call me eccentric, but I say if the only way we can eliminate every last weed is to poison the earth with some of the most deadly substances known to science, then let's just have a few weeds, huh? I quite like dandelions and groundsel and purple headed thistles.

And then what does our gardener do, having killed the weed? In its place he plants a little innocent leafy green plant which thrusts its tender shoots trustingly up toward that kissing sun. But it's his plant, you see. A horticultural mutant, unknown in Nature, and unable to survive without further aggressive measures against the natural world by its jealous owner and guardian. So the regiments of insecticides and fungicides are brought in to play, to complement the battalions of herbicides.

So enter dichlorophen, benomyl, malathion, carbendazim and others. And if you had any doubts, the trade names these are sold under leave you in no doubt that gardening is war! Murphy Systematic Insecticide. Boots Ant Destroyer. Murphy Tumblebug. Wasp-End. I.C.I. Super Bug Gun. This is 'Come out with your feelers up!' stuff.

And this just demonstrates the fatuity of that line about the birds. Those much loved mirthful wild birds eat slug pellets and are poisoned by them. Song thrushes suffer particularly badly. The insect-eating robins can't find enough insects to eat in the garden. Green woodpeckers will not visit a garden bereft of ants. Ants are a major component of their diet.

The other side of gardening is nurturing the plants you have planted. Again, this is not for the squeamish. From the slaughterhouse we get dried blood, bone meal and hoof and horn. From the sea we get fishmeal. And from the farm we get manure. It is intriguing to reflect that if the vegetarians have their way, these products will no longer be available, and it is they who rely the most on the products of the kitchen garden. Alternatively, of course, there are mineral or 'artificial' fertilisers such as phosphates and nitrates which are mined and quarried, but these are the subject of controversial arguments about pollution and despoliation of the environment. So eat meat and save the planet!

But our brave gardener is not finished yet. He has a lawn!

Maintaining a lawn must rank with golf as one of the most futile exercises known to man. You plant grass seed. You feed it with Lawn Green to make it grow. You zap all other plant life with Supertox Lawn Weed Spray, and Murphy Super Moss Killer and Fungicide. Then you spend up to several hundred quid on a contraption which has no other purpose than to cut the carefully nurtured grass. And then what do you do with this hard won harvest? You throw it away. And then you pile on more Lawn Green to make it grow again.

Admittedly, a few enlightened gardeners are at last realising that God didn't get it all wrong after all. So they are planting wild flower seeds. Then they wonder how they can tell the difference between the wild flowers which came out of their seed packet, and the weeds, i.e. the wild flowers which just grew -er wild, as it were. This question was actually asked of a local newspaper gardening column recently. The questioner was solemnly counselled to familiarise himself with the 'common weeds' of the area, and then get an illustrated book of wild flowers 'to see what the stems or leaves of your flowers should look like.' The logic of this can only have been that a wild flower which was not in the wild flower book was not a wild flower, especially if it happened to be a wild flower common to the district!

But my bête noir is the rose. I loathe roses. They are totally functionless and artificial. They have no reproductive ability and no pollen or nectar, so they are useless to bees and butterflies. They have no rootstock, and have to be grafted on to the briar rose root. Rose bushes are thorny and unsightly, and have to be pruned and dead-headed regularly just to make them flower and look reasonable. And they need prodigious quantities of horseshi- erm, manure.

Somebody once asked my father what he would like for the garden. 'Six tons of concrete' came the prompt reply. He has passed all his love of gardening on to me.

"The sun cannot give you pardon
For wantonly killing the Earth.
You can kick God out of your garden
But how much is that garden then worth?"

© 2004 Paul Winstanley

PRICKLY PROBLEM

"You have so little empathy for the feelings of women." Thus spake my daughter, following yet another failure by me to comprehend some relationship problem or other or what seemed to me to be a mere capricious tantrum. "It's a wonder I have any empathy at all" I say, defensively. "I am of the Roy Rogers generation, you know." I expect this to mean something to her. But I expect in vain. "Roy Who?" is the certain reply.

You have to be of a certain age to remember Roy Rogers. He was the king of the singing cowboys who thrilled us kids at Saturday morning cinema. It strikes me now that his character in the films must have been possessed of a good private income, as he never seemed to have to do any work. He just wandered round the Wild West like a check-shirted knight-errant, meeting with the beautiful daughters of old ranchers who were having trouble with baddies. In between shooting up the baddies, he found time to strum his guitar and sing a couple of songs about the lone prairie to the adoring daughter. But he never actually got her, not even a kiss. He just rode off into the sunset carolling about tumbleweed.

And when you heard his theme song, "A Four-Legged Friend," which was a kind of hymn to his horse, you understood why. The man was a raving misogynist! The second verse of "A Four-Legged Friend" went like this:

'A woman's like cactus, and cactus can hurt
For she's just a tight-waisted winking-eyed flirt!
She'll have all your money, your lands and your gold
And bury you deep long before you grow old.'

The chorus then informed you that by contrast a four legged friend, a four legged friend, he'll never let you down, he'll be honest and faithful right up to the end, 'that wonderful one two three four legged friend' just in case you still hadn't quite grasped the essential quadrupedality of this -er companion, or friend, as it were.

Now just what was a simple eight-year-old country lad, with several years to go before puberty, to make of all this? Why should the number of legs vary in direct proportion to the quality of friendship? Was it applicable only to horses, or would a six or eight-legged friend be even better than a four-legged one?

But it was the unfavourable comparison of two-legged women, but not two-legged men, with the four-legged horse that was so mystifying. Maybe women were some kind of two-legged horse. After all, Rogers didn't have a verse in his song against male two legged friends, although he didn't seem actually to have any himself. He didn't have a sidekick, like the Lone Ranger had Tonto, and he sure wasn't like Hopalong Cassidy, who had all his pards from the 6T6 Ranch. So perhaps it was O.K. to have your mates, but a horse would be better if only you could get one. I had no way of testing this, as I hadn't got a horse. My concept of a four-legged friend was more likely to be a dog or a cat, or even a frog or a mouse. But even I could tell that that was not quite what Roy Rogers had in mind. The one clear message however was that you must avoid these gold-grabbing cactus-prickly women at all costs.

Of course, what puzzles an eight-year-old does not trouble a fifteen-year-old. By then I had made great strides in my education, including the pleasurable discovery, from hands-on experience, that girls were not really like cactus at all.

But by the standards of today I was, and still am, a total innocent. I am full of envy for today's sexually enlightened youngsters. Most of them attend comprehensive schools, and even those who don't are not brought up to believe that the opposite sex is an alien species, as we were.

An exaggeration? I don't think so. Firstly, we were sorted into two distinct sexual groups by the eleven plus examination, something the legislators of 1944 no doubt did not contemplate. Those of us who passed it went to grammar schools which were invariably single sex. Those who did not pass it went to secondary modern schools which were nearly always for both sexes, or 'co-educational' as it was called. The inference, to my callow mind, seemed to be that intellectual types, destined for illustrious careers, must maintain their academic purity by putting all fleshly thoughts aside and concentrating on their latin irregular verbs, while the future hewers of wood and drawers of water in the secondary moderns could be allowed to neglect their less demanding studies and take time out to have it off behind their co-educational bike-sheds.

This idea was reinforced by the grammar schools. The attitude to sex at my own school was virtually monastic. There was, for example, a written rule which forbade us to talk to girls in the street whilst in school uniform. The enforcement of this rule often led to ludicrous situations, since one of the few excuses accepted, if anyone were challenged by a prefect or master, was that you were talking to your sister. It is amazing how many brothers the local girls had!

All this inculcated within us a most peculiar concept of women, as creatures not to be taken seriously and best avoided altogether by good clean-living lads. And goodness knows what attitudes toward men it led to in girls, who were no less rigorously segregated.

And then my family wonder about my ignorance of women? It's just as well we never had horses. I might have ended up marrying one.

© 2004 Paul Winstanley

THE SAFETY VALVE

"That must have been the worst meal you have ever produced in the whole of our married life." I was emptying the remains of the meal, about 90% of the meal actually, into the waste bin after our dinner party, and began to warm to my theme. "No-one wanted any second helpings. They couldn't even finish their first helpings. There was more left on their plates when they finished than when they first started. My jaw still aches from trying to chew that duck. What on earth was it? A rubber one from the bathroom? And it was only Trevor and I who could even attempt the potatoes, and he's an engineer. What did you do? Case-harden them in a furnace?" I looked for some signs of contrition and suitably abashed humility from the wifely person.

"I did them the new French way."

"Oh, well, that explains it. Now we know where they get their boules from then, don't we! Who needs metal when you can get petrified tuber! Not so much pommes frites as pommes de fonte." Unfortunately as she doesn't speak French this brilliant witticism was wasted.

She looked at me, quite unabashed. "It's not the worst we've ever had. Remember the apple turnovers!"

"Oh, well. If you're going to count the apple turnovers....." This was, of course, blatant cheating. I could not maintain my righteous indignation if she was going to bring in the saga of the apple turnovers. It always made us laugh, as my wife, cunning minx, had known it would. Ah, yes, the apple turnovers. Well I mind the day etc. etc..

We had been married barely three weeks. My new wife had been brought up in the rustic 'feed-the-brute' school of cookery, designed to assuage the ravenous appetites of rugby-playing farmworkers, and she had not yet adjusted to the more refined requirements of a desk-bound couch potato. So one evening, after two helpings of steak-and-kidney pudding with dumplings, turnips and and mashed, ('sure you can't manage any more?') she proudly produced the apple turnovers together with a large jug of custard. There were just two of the turnovers, rather bigger than previous specimens I had seen, and each filled a large plate.

I undid my top button, smiled dutifully across at the beloved and attacked the pastry. It soon became obvious that the puny utensils from our new wedding present canteen of cutlery were not going to be equal to the task. Putting aside the bent fork, I suggested we use the serrated steak-knives. But after two minutes steady sawing I had only managed to make the faintest of grooves in the pastry plating. My beloved had given up and was near to tears.

"Perhaps it wasn't the right flour." she snivelled.

"Sure it wasn't Grade A cement?" I said, trying to cheer her up.

She remained uncheered, while I gallantly tried hammering at the unyielding carapace with the steak tenderizer.

"If only we'd got an electric carving knife. But nobody gave us one." wailed the beloved.

I reflected that no-one had given us a jack hammer or a pneumatic concrete breaker either. The beloved burst into tears.

"They'll have to go in the bin." I said finally. This met with a howl of protest, and it occurred to me that we could face prosecution for sabotaging the shredding and crushing plant. In the end we decided to bury the turnovers in the garden.

It was a simple but moving ceremony, the beloved kneeling in her pinafore to lay to rest the apples in their impermeable coffins next to the forget-me-nots. A little girl next door, assuming we must be burying a family pet, generously yanked up several of her father's prize gladioli and solemnly passed them over to us. I opened my mouth to explain, but words failed me. "That's alright!" she said kindly, obviously thinking me overcome with emotion. Under her expectant gaze, we put the flowers on the grave and stood, feeling rather foolish. I wondered whether the turnovers would rot or fossilise, and, if the latter, what archaeologists a thousand years hence might make of them. No doubt they would conclude that they were offerings to propitiate the gods after a bad apple harvest.

But the valedictory vigil could not last long. We could not keep our faces straight. Leaving the little girl still peering er - gravely, as it were, over the fence, we scuttled back indoors and collapsed into fits of uncontrollable giggles. At length we dried our eyes, washed up and went early to bed. Well, we were newly-weds after all.

And of course, that is what we did now, some twenty-odd years later, in the wake of the rubber duck and concrete potatoes, but this time I did not have to get up frantically in the middle of the night to retrieve the gladioli from the grave before our neighbour saw them. Every couple should have an apple turnovers incident in their lives. It might even save some marriages.

© 2004 Paul Winstanley

DEADLIER THAN THE MALE
Set in Tudor times, around the year 1500
Not for the squeamish!

The first insipid rays of the winter sun illuminated the hoar-frost which thickly encrusted the grass of the courtyard in front of the castle. It sparkled on the leafless tree branches, and it even lent a strange beauty to the hempen rope of the six nooses which dangled from the gibbett in the centre of the yard, around which pressed a crowd of watchers who had been assembling for the past two hours. The executioner, a large crop-haired man, barechested despite the cold, was making final adjustments to the ropes. He had two assistants, one of whom was lighting an iron brazier full of charcoal, while the other sharpened the axe and knives ready for the quartering. Between the watchers and the gibbett a line of halbardiers stood facing the crowd, their faces impassive, their weapons at the present, breastplates gleaming dully in the watery sunlight.

The heavy iron-studded door of the castle crashed open. The crowd fell silent and still, craning their necks to see. First came the Captain of the Castle Guard from the darkness of the interior, followed by two guardsmen, then a bare-headed priest in a white surplice, carrying a crucifix and a heavy book. Behind him four attendants bore a gilt-edged canopy under which walked the magistrate in a flowing scarlet cloak. Behind him, shuffling as they were pushed forward by four more guardsmen, followed the six prisoners who had been condemned to death. Their hands were bound behind their backs.

The little procession walked toward the gibbett, where the executioners' assistants waited to take charge of the prisoners.

Suddenly there was a commotion as a scuffle broke out amongst the crowd. The soldiers moved to quell the disturbance and, taking advantage of this distraction, a woman in a long cloak broke through the line and ran toward one of the prisoners.

Two guards turned and suddenly noticing her moved back to intercept her.

"Stand away, woman. No-one may approach the prisoners."

"I wish only to bid farewell to the man I love"

The guard hesitated momentarily but still shook his head.

"Surely it will cost naught for us to say goodbye." It was the prisoner who spoke.

"Silence!" The guard struck him across the face. "Your whore can bid you farewell as you dance on the rope's end." He turned to the woman. "Get back!"

"What is amiss here?" It was the Captain.

"I wish only to say farewell to my beloved, Captain." The woman pulled her hood back and opened her cloak. She was tall and strongly built, her body rounded and statuesque.

The big soldier licked his lip and hesitated.

The woman's gaze moved from the Captain to the magistrate, who in turn regarded her intently. The woman's nod was barely perceptible. The faintest smirk appeared on the magistrate's face.

"It will do no harm, Captain."

"Very well. Quickly."

The woman embraced her lover passionately, and with a total lack of self-consciousness kissed him full and lingeringly on the mouth. After a few seconds the Captain growled "Enough!"

She pulled back as her arms released their embrace and cupped her hands tenderly round his face.

"Goodbye, Daniel my own true love." she whispered.

The prisoner's lips had barely mouthed "Goodbye" when the heel of her hand slipped swiftly over his mouth. The other hand clamped the side of his face, as in one movement she twisted and wrenched his head violently up and sideways. There was a loud crack as his neck bones broke. His body shuddered briefly, then went limp as she caught his waist and laid him gently to the ground.

A soft murmur broke from the astonished crowd. The Captain stood in shock for a moment, then rushed toward the prostrate prisoner. One glance was enough. The head was twisted at an unnatural angle, the eyes staring, and a large purple patch had appeared on the neck. He gave the corpse a furious kick, then turned to the woman.

He spluttered at her incoherently, finally managing just one word. "Why?"

"Do you think I wanted to see my lover's heart torn from his breast and held aloft by yonder villain?" Her voice was clear and fearless. "I could not save him, but his death was clean."

"Bind her arms." snapped the Captain to the guards.

"You have saved your lover's pains. So you shall have the privilege of suffering in his stead."

He moved towards her. His hand reached out and and tore down the front of her gown, exposing her full creamy breasts.

"Heat the tongs!" he barked to the executioner's assistant. The man thrust a pair of hooked three-pointed tongs deep into the charcoal, and his fellow torturer blew the coals into redness with a bellows.

A terrified gasp broke from the woman's throat. She looked at the brutalised faces of the peasant mob, slavering at the prospect of what was to come, at the pitiless expressions of the soldiers, and then, desperately and expectantly, at the magistrate, who stood, wordless. Her hand went briefly to her exposed nipple.

The magistrate at last spoke. "Just what do you imagine you are doing, Captain?"

The Captain spat viciously. "She is a harlot! A witch! Those pretty dugs shall be ripped from her carcase with hot irons. The rack shall tear those arms from their shoulder sockets."

"A little late for that, don't you think, Captain?" His voice was mocking and cruel. "Those arms have already done their work and cheated the noose and the knife."

"She must be put to the torture." said the Captain, sullenly.

"That will be for me to decide, Captain." said the magistrate. "But don't you think you have a more urgent problem?"

The big man stopped, puzzled.

"Sir Richard de Vere will attend here soon, and he has waited long to see this day. He will expect to see six prisoners brought to the King's justice, not five. What will we say to him? That a whore tricked you?"

The Captain's expression of anger gave way to panic.

The magistrate's voice became silky and menacing. "It was your duty to deliver the prisoners to justice. Yours and mine. We are accountable to Sir Richard. You have failed in that duty, Captain. You have failed me. You have neglected your duty. And what is the penalty for dereliction of duty?"

The magistrate's languid demeanour suddenly changed. He turned to two of the guards. "Your Captain is under arrest. Secure him." The men hesitated. "Quickly, unless you all want to wear a hempen collar." This put an end to their hesitation.

"Strip him." said the magistrate.

"And you two. Get the clothes off this piece of carrion and put them on him." It was soon done. The Captain struggled and shouted, but his protests were ignored, and a blow to the head with a heavy mace quietened him. Soon he stood in the dead prisoner's clothes. The body was dragged away out of sight.

"So this is how you reward loyal service. I always served you well!" said the Captain.

"And you will serve me well now." came the reply "I shall show Sir Richard six executions this day."

The Captain was defiant. "You were present here when the witch struck. Why should I take all blame? When Sir Richard comes, you shall find I have a tongue in my head."

The magistrate suddenly became very still. "So you have." he said softly. Then, to the guards "Put him on his knees."

The magistrate drew a small bone-handled dagger. "Open his mouth!"

The captain cried and struggled desperately, but another blow with the mace half-stunned him. His jaw was wrenched open. The magistrate's eyes were blue chips of ice, his mouth a thin merciless line as he quickly inserted the blade into the Captain's mouth, then cut, twisted and turned. A murmur of surprise and awe arose from the crowd, who pressed forward as far as the halberdiers would allow. This was an unexpected bonus on their entertainment. The Captain roared with agony as the magistrate's hand wrenched a pulsating lump of bleeding flesh from his mouth and threw it on the ground. Two mangy village dogs leapt upon it.

The magistrate removed his bloodstained leather gauntlets and flung them with distaste at one of the guards. Meanwhile the Captain had been hauled back to his feet. He stood, swaying slightly between the two men who held him, gurgling groans coming from his blood-streaming mouth.

The sound of hoofbeats came clearly through the frosty air, as three horsemen galloped across the castle green. The leader was clad in light armour and mail, over which he wore a surcoat bearing the royal arms. The other two wore plain chain mail, and one of them led another horse tethered behind his own, saddled but with no rider.

They rode up to the line of soldiers. "Let me pass, in the name of the King." said the leader. His companions followed.

The leader looked down, unsmiling. "I seek Magistrate Goodfellow."

"I am he."

"I am the King's Messenger. I have a stay of execution for Daniel Harcourt. You are to release him now into my custody."

The magistrate was puzzled. "How may this be? Is he then pardoned?"

"He is to be questioned further. That is all I know" He turned his horse toward the prisoners. "Well, which is Daniel Harcourt?"

The Captain made an incoherent noise, and nodded desperately toward the magistrate. Blood poured from his mouth.

"Is that he? What has happened to him?

"He has been put to the statutory torture."

"Then he had better be questioned quickly, while he yet lives." said the king's messenger indifferently. "Loose his bonds. He must ride with us."

The magistrate opened his mouth as if to say something, but then closed it, hesitated, and finally nodded to a guard, who cut the rope binding the Captain's wrists.

The magistrate turned back to speak to the messenger, but before he could say anything the Captain let out a snarling growl and launched himself at the magistrate. Both men fell to the ground, blood gouting from the Captain's mouth and spattering both men as they wrestled on the ground. Despite his wounds the big soldier was far stronger than the soft-living magistrate, and soon had him pinned him to the ground. The Captain's blood drenched the magistrate's face as he opened his mouth, wrenched back the magistrate's head and bit deeply into his exposed throat.

It took all the guards and two soldiers to pull the hate-crazed captain off the magistrate. By the time they hauled the captain to his feet the magistrate lay twisted and unmoving, dark crimson blood gushing from a gash in his throat, staining the scarlet of his robes and melting the frost on the grass. The captain spat out a piece of flesh, and roared in triumph. The crowd gave a cheer. They had no love for magistrates.

The messenger dismounted. He looked in disbelief at the captain. "Why in the name of heaven did you do that? Are you Daniel Harcourt?"

The captain shook his head and tried to speak. But all that came from his mouth was a groan, which turned to a gurgling splutter as the lifeblood heamorrhaged from his mouth. Finally his legs gave way, and he crashed to the ground, shivered and and lay still.

The messenger looked at the guards. "Who in God's name is in command here? Where is your Captain?"

One of the men pointed to the prone figure in front of them. The messenger looked down at the blood-soaked corpse, then back at the guards. Speechless. Uncomprehending.

"It was that woman." stammered one at length.

"What woman?"

All eyes now turned to look for the dark-haired woman who had wrought such havoc, but she was nowhere to be seen.

© 2004 Paul Winstanley

PAINTBALLS AND FLOWER BASKETS

A dear friend wrote to me recently 'I am quite the social animal at the moment but I do not live it. I experience it.' That statement intrigued me. What on earth did it mean? Then I found myself reminded of those words during a subsequent evening spent with neighbours.

Now the point of visiting neighbours, or indeed of visiting anybody, is to talk. Admittedly there might be a bit of decent food and drink, and the women in particular can rubber-neck at the decor and the curtains and gather enough visual data to fuel conversations on the way home. You know the sort of thing, whether their sitting room is quite as big as ours and it's obvious that wall unit doesn't go with the three-piece. ('Didn't you really notice that awful vase!) But these are peripheral amusements. It is for the conversation that we undertake social visiting.

At least, it should be. Dr. Samuel Johnson, he who singlehandedly wrote the first English dictionary and who was arguably one of the biggest gasbags in history said "That is the happiest conversation where there is no competition, no vanity, but a calm quiet interchange of sentiments." Quite so, dear Doctor. But it's not always like that.

We were all retirees from the London area, and the quite laudable idea of our hostess was that we get to know each other. Well, I suppose that is what happened.

The topic which seemed to occupy almost totally the mind of the lady I was first sitting next to was hanging flower baskets. She used to have a lot of hanging flower baskets. Everyone had hanging flower baskets in her street, and there were plant nurseries in the area famed far and wide for the quality and infinite variety of their hanging flower baskets. Apparently not all plants were suitable for hanging flower baskets. Some of them don't hang properly, you see. I felt myself flagging and consciously bolstered my concentration. Hanging flower baskets are very interesting. They are. Really. Obviously we were privileged to have the hanging flower basket doyenne of north London here. She herself did not buy ready made hanging flower baskets of course but always planted up her own. I quickly picked up on the 'of course' and said 'Ahahah!' and nodded sagely. I was rather proud of that. I nodded again as she told me that fibre was better than moss for planting hanging flower baskets, and nodded and ahah'd even more as she explained in detail the watering techniques required. Apparently there is a special type of watering can, recognisable only to the discerning, and only by the use of that particular utensil can the irrigation of hanging flower baskets be adequately performed. By this time my neck muscles were aching and I must have resembled the nodding porcelain Chinese mandarin my mother had had on the mantle-shelf, which she would lift me up to demonstrate in my infant years.

Fortunately at that point the lady decided she should help the hostess with the food. I turned with but short-lived relief to the man on my right, for it became quickly apparent that he was no less of a monomaniac. His passion was paintballing. He had paintballed in Wales. He had paintballed in the New Forest. He had paintballed in France and in Germany and Luxemburg. 'Even Luxemburg?' I said, fixing my face with my special Rivettingly Interested look. Unfortunately he wasn't quite so good at filling conversational lacunae as Hanging Basket Woman, and I had to think up some responses. 'Have you ever been to Lanzarote?' I said, thinking I could tell him about the little lizards I had found there, and thus open up a natural history front to the discourse. But he hadn't been to Lanzarote. He frowned. The terrain wouldn't really be suitable for paintballing would it. No I guessed it wouldn't. Silly of me to ask really.

As the evening wore on Paintball Man formed an alliance with another obsessive, Outward Bound and Orienteering Man, and the pair launched into what sounded like a competition to see who could make his hobby sound the most unappealing. "I had bruises for three weeks .... never has cold porridge and irish stew tasted so delicious .... he still walks with a limp .... this swamp reeked like dead cats .... he got to the middle and then said 'I can't swim' .... I'm sure that's why I get this pain even now.......... we thought he was a gonner" and so on and so bloody on. I was reminded of the how-I-won-the-war stories men used to regale schoolboys with in my boyhood. Just what was I doing here? I was even starting to pine for Hanging Basket Woman, whose discourse at least had some purpose but who now seemed to be holding my wife enthralled.

Finally the dread moment. 'What do you do with yourself then, mate!' said Orienteering Man. What on earth to say?

'Erm, a bit of writing' I stuttered.

'Oh yeah. What do you write then? Anything any good? How many books have you published? Do you know Andy McNab? I knew this bloke who was a bit of a writer. Shot an Abominable Snowman in Nepal and sold the film rights of the book for three million ....'

I tried again. 'I'm interested in family History.'

'Oh yeah. Did you see that program about this bloke who reckons his great grandad owned Manhattan Island? And I knew this geezer once who said if only he could prove it, his uncle could be the King of Sweden ....'

My mind started wandering uncontrollably. I envisioned Paintball Man firing paintballs at hanging flower baskets. Oh Dr Johnson, what would you have made of this lot? Maybe it was different in your day. A lot of things were. Perhaps we just don't do calm quiet interchanges of sentiments in the twenty-first century.

© 2004 Paul Winstanley

A COVER-UP JOB

Why do we wear clothes? The answer to that question, in the context of modern society and climate, might seem obvious. But why do we? How on earth did it all begin?

It seems to me that the first garment ever made, the very first piece of mammoth-skin, or whatever, to be cut and twisted into something resembling an item of clothing and put upon the human person, must surely have been invented by a woman. No man would ever have inflicted such a scourge upon the human race.

As far as I know, no serious research has actually been done into which of the sexes is actually to blame for clothes. Even Genesis dodges it, having both Adam and Eve simultaneously reaching for the fig-leaves. But I'll bet it was Eve. "For goodness sake put something on!" she will have said, handing Adam a leaf. A very large leaf of course.

Things have progressed, or degenerated, depending upon your view, massively since that leaf. But it is still women who instinctively know about clothes, and it is they who draw up the ground rules. Men learn these rules only by blundering against them.

And it is not only his own clothes the unwary male must worry about. Pitfalls abound, especially when he is trying some gambit from the 'How to keep your Marriage Fresh' book.

"That's a nice dress! Haven't seen that before." he says, remembering the Attentiveness bit from page 14. "Oh for goodness sake, I've had this for ages!" comes the reply. "Don't you remember? I wore it to Stephanie's party." Now with luck, Stephanie's party wasn't just last week, or he is really in dead trouble. Quite probably it was over a year ago. And she can not only remember what she herself wore, but what he wore, and what everybody else wore that night. On the other hand, if he remembers the party at all, it will not be the women's clothes he remembers. Well, not their colour anyway.

But it is clothes nostalgia which is the most dangerous ground for the male. Conversations evoking memories of engagement evenings, weddings (especially one's own) and romantic holidays. "You looked absolutely gorgeous!" he will say. Safe enough comment, he may think. Not much chance of contradiction there. "I'll bet you don't remember, really." comes the reply. Then she delivers the killer. "What was I wearing then?" Ah! Well -erm. That red thing? And of course, it wasn't, was it. It was that pale turquoise thing with a black bolero jacket.. How could it possibly not be indelibly etched in his memory? And when it comes to the wedding! Someone should advise every newly-wed male to make careful note of what the beloved wore to 'go away' in, and keep it safe. It could save the marriage some ten or twenty years later.

But when it comes to his own clothes, the problems really kick in for the average male. First you have to acquire them. Casual clothes are bad enough, but as soon as you start getting formal, into suit territory, it becomes painfully apparent that the western lounge suit is the most impractical abomination ever invented. The human form is a wonderful thing. It moves and bends. The bottom half does not lend itself to being stuffed into two cloth tubes joined together at one of the most sensitive areas we possess. And as for the top half, it's hopeless. The shoulder joint is one of the most flexible parts in the human body. You only have to stretch out your arm for the sleeve to look ridiculous. The Arab jellabah or even the Roman toga would make far more sense.

But we all have to wear a suit at some time or other, which means we have to go through the process of buying it. Most men try to get away with ready-made. The process of bespoke tailoring must be one of the worst ordeals ever contrived. It's worse than having your hair cut, and almost as bad as visiting the dentist's. For whilst a shop assistant will fit you until you are satisfied, the bespoke tailor will fit you until he is satisfied, which means that he will continue until long after you have lost all interest, and feel like screaming. But you have to stand there, looking in those mirrors on all sides of the cubicle, while they cut the stitches of sleeves and collars, pin and re-pin and underpin, and make mysterious signs and symbols with chalk, as if you were being prepared for some occult ritual. You note with distaste your spreading midriff, your sloping shoulders and your thinning hair. Full face is bad enough, but your profile is worse and as for your back view ....! Then they tell you that they must have another fitting next week. And it's only a jacket and trousers, for goodness sake!

But even off-the-peg is not without its trauma. Thanks to the female sex. What man has not suffered the indignity of buying clothes under the supervision of the woman in his life? Aside from the old cliché about being made to try on everything in the shop and then ending up buying the item he first put on, it is such an indignity. And the shop assistants hone their comments with exquisite malignity, inevitably using a mocking royal plural. "We are more inclining to the Portly now, I think, Sir. We were Regular once, maybe, but yes, I really do think the Portly." The Beloved, meanwhile, sits on a chair like a theatre impressario turning down hopeful new acts. "No. Now let's see that one. Oh, no. And that. Oh good gracious, no! What about that other one? Oh, certainly not! Not with your colouring."

And even then, having finally got us to buy something of which they approve, our dear ladies must prescribe how we wear it. The first of these rules is epitomised by "You can't possibly wear that with that. What? Why? "Don't be silly. Go and put on your other one." comes the reply. Finally the luckless male is shoved and pulled into some shirt or jacket he'd forgotten he had, which has become too small and which is either too light or heavy for the time of year. But it's the right colour, you see.

"Why can't you wear your clothes properly?" the beloved will say, pulling at the collar, or jacket lapels, and yanking at your tie. "Why do all your jackets go out of shape so?" A withering appraisal of one's torso follows, accompanied by critical prods and jabs. Well, one reason might be that a man cannot put all the necessary impedimenta of modern living into a hand-bag the way women can. Let a woman try carrying a wallet, cheque-book, diary, keys, loose change, handkerchief, ball-point pen and possibly cigarettes and lighter all in her tailored designer suit, and see what shape that ends up in. She'd have more to worry about than whether her bum looked big. And other parts might not look big enough in competition with the new bulges.

And don't tell me that male handbags are available. They are indeed, and what did the wifely person say, when I tried one? "You're not walking down the street with me like that!" Mind you, I'm rather glad she did. Even one's own sex will form unfavourable and totally unjustified impressions of men who wear 'ponce-bags.' Bum-bags of course are acceptable in totally naff situations, such as with shorts and tee-shirt in Torremolinos, but that's about as far as we can go.

It seems to me that buying, choosing and wearing clothes properly must be a full-time job, leaving no room for anything else in your life. To look neat and spruce, avoiding bagging trousers and sagging jackets, must involve never carrying anything much other than a silk hankie, never sitting down, never going out in the rain and never perspiring. Maybe tailors themselves can do it. The old adage about nine tailors making a man must have some significance.

© 2004 Paul Winstanley